Contents

Introduction

In the ever-evolving landscape of Information Technology (IT), the ability to effectively manage problems and disruptions is paramount. In a world where digital services underpin nearly every aspect of our lives, the resolution of IT issues can make the difference between seamless operations and costly downtime. This is where ITIL Problem Management comes into play, offering a systematic and proven approach to identifying, addressing, and ultimately preventing recurring issues.

The world of ITIL (IT Infrastructure Library) has long been a guiding light for organizations striving to deliver high-quality IT services. ITIL provides a comprehensive framework of best practices for IT Service Management, offering a structured and efficient way to meet the challenges of the digital age.

This book, "Mastering ITIL Problem Management: Setting Up and Optimization," is your essential companion on the journey to becoming a proficient and successful ITIL Problem Manager. It is designed to help you navigate the intricacies of ITIL Problem Management, from its foundational principles to advanced strategies for optimizing your problem-solving processes.

The Importance of Problem Management

In the IT world, problems and incidents are inevitable. Systems will fail, services will experience disruptions, and errors will occur. How an organization responds to these issues can make all the difference in its ability to maintain smooth operations and satisfy customers. Problem Management is the key to not only resolving these issues but also preventing them from reoccurring in the future. It's about tackling the root causes, not just the symptoms, of IT disruptions.

By implementing robust Problem Management practices, organizations can:

1. Reduce Downtime: Promptly identifying and resolving problems minimizes service downtime, ensuring that businesses can operate smoothly without costly interruptions.

2. Enhance Customer Satisfaction: Reliable services result in satisfied customers who can trust your organization to meet their needs.

3. Optimize Resource Allocation: Problem Management allows for better allocation of resources, as IT teams can focus on solving critical issues rather than repeatedly firefighting the same problems.

4. Foster Continuous Improvement: Through careful analysis and root cause identification, Problem Management paves the way for ongoing service improvement and better decision-making.

Goals of the Book

This book is your comprehensive guide to Problem Management, whether you're just beginning your journey or seeking to optimize an existing problem management framework. Here's what you can expect to gain from reading and applying the knowledge within:

1. Understanding the Fundamentals: You will gain a solid understanding of ITIL and the role of Problem Management within IT Service Management. We will cover the essential concepts, terminology, and principles that underpin this discipline.

2. Setting Up Problem Management: We will guide you through the process of establishing Problem Management within your organization. This includes defining processes, assembling a team, identifying key stakeholders, and creating policies to guide your efforts.

3. Effective Problem-Solving: You will learn best practices for problem identification, logging, categorization, prioritization, investigation, and resolution. These are the building blocks of successful Problem Management.

4. Continuous Improvement: We will explore how to foster a culture of continuous improvement, with a focus on knowledge management, metrics, and key performance indicators (KPIs) that enable you to measure and enhance your Problem Management processes.

5. Real-World Insights: Throughout the book, you will find case studies and examples from leading organizations, illustrating successful Problem Management implementations, challenges faced, and lessons learned.

6. Future-Ready: We will discuss emerging trends and technologies in Problem Management, ensuring you are well-prepared to adapt to the ever-changing IT landscape.

How to Use This Book

"Mastering ITIL Problem Management" is designed to be both a structured learning resource and a practical guide. Whether you're an IT professional, manager, or executive, you can navigate through the chapters based on your specific needs and goals. You can use this book as a step-by-step manual to set up and optimize Problem Management practices, or as a reference guide to tackle specific issues as they arise in your IT environment.

So, whether you're just beginning your journey into ITIL Problem Management or looking to refine your existing practices, welcome to the world of efficient problem-solving, continuous improvement, and the power to deliver resilient, high-quality IT services. Let's embark on this journey together, and, by the end, you'll be well on your way to mastering ITIL Problem Management.

Fundamentals of Problem Management

Problem Management is a fundamental component of ITIL, a framework that has become the gold standard for IT Service Management. In this chapter, we'll delve into the core principles and concepts that underpin Problem Management, providing you with a strong foundation to build upon.

Understanding ITIL and Its Components

Before we dive deep into Problem Management, it's crucial to grasp the broader context of ITIL. ITIL, or IT Infrastructure Library, is a comprehensive set of best practices designed to help organizations align their IT services with the needs of the business. At its core, ITIL consists of several key components, including:

1. Service Strategy: This component helps define an IT organization's overall service strategy and how it can meet business objectives.

2. Service Design: It focuses on the design of IT services, ensuring they align with business goals and are cost-effective.

3. Service Transition: This phase addresses the transition of new or modified services into operation while minimizing disruption.

4. Service Operation: The component that manages services in a live environment, including Incident Management, Change Management, and, of course, Problem Management.

5. Continual Service Improvement: This component emphasizes the need for ongoing evaluation and improvement of IT services.

Problem Management fits into the Service Operation phase, specifically addressing the handling of problems and ensuring the smooth operation of IT services.

What Is Problem Management?

Problem Management, in the context of ITIL, is a systematic approach to identifying, documenting, and resolving underlying causes of incidents to prevent them from recurring. It's not about quick fixes but rather about finding permanent solutions to IT disruptions.

Key points to understand about Problem Management:

- Proactive vs. Reactive: Problem Management is proactive, focusing on preventing incidents before they occur, rather than merely reacting to them.

- Incident vs. Problem: While Incident Management focuses on restoring services as quickly as possible, Problem Management looks deeper to understand why incidents occur and how to prevent their recurrence.

- Efficiency and Reliability: Problem Management is about improving the efficiency and reliability of IT services by addressing underlying issues that may lead to incidents.

Key Concepts and Terminology

Problem Management has its own set of key concepts and terminology. Understanding these is essential for effective communication and implementation of Problem Management processes:

1. Problem: A problem is an underlying cause of one or more incidents. It's not the incident itself but the issue that needs to be addressed to prevent similar incidents.

2. Known Error: A known error is a problem that has been identified, analyzed, and documented, but a solution has not yet been implemented.

3. Root Cause: The root cause is the fundamental reason for a problem. It's what needs to be addressed to prevent recurring incidents.

4. Workaround: A workaround is a temporary solution that allows services to be restored quickly while the root cause is being addressed.

5. Error Control Process: This process is responsible for managing known errors and ensuring that they are resolved through the Problem Management process.

6. Problem Model: A problem model is a template or framework for documenting problems, making it easier to identify, analyze, and resolve them.

The Role of Problem Management in IT Service Management

Problem Management plays a vital role in the broader IT Service Management framework. Here's why it's so important:

- Ensuring Service Quality: By addressing the root causes of incidents, Problem Management contributes to the delivery of reliable and high-quality IT services.

- Cost Savings: Effective Problem Management reduces the time and resources spent on recurring incidents, resulting in cost savings for the organization.

- Customer Satisfaction: Fewer incidents and disruptions mean happier customers and end-users who can rely on your services.

- Knowledge Sharing: Problem Management creates a knowledge base of known errors and solutions, facilitating knowledge sharing and continuous improvement.

Now that we've covered the fundamentals, we're ready to explore the process of setting up Problem Management in the following chapter. From defining processes to assembling your team and creating policies, we'll guide you through the essential steps to get started with Problem Management in your organization.

Organizational Readiness for Problem Management

In the realm of ITIL Problem Management, organizational readiness is the first crucial step toward establishing a robust and effective process. To ensure that Problem Management can function optimally within your organization, it's essential to assess, plan, and adapt your environment to align with the principles and practices of Problem Management. In this chapter, we'll explore the concept of organizational readiness and provide you with a comprehensive guide on how to prepare your organization for the successful implementation of Problem Management.

Understanding Organizational Readiness

Organizational readiness, in the context of Problem Management, refers to an organization's preparedness to effectively implement and manage Problem Management processes. This readiness encompasses several critical aspects that need to be evaluated and addressed before you embark on the journey of establishing Problem Management. It ensures that the organization is equipped with the necessary resources, commitment, and culture to support this important ITIL discipline.

Why Is Organizational Readiness Important?

Implementing Problem Management successfully requires more than just adopting a new set of procedures and practices. It necessitates an alignment of people, processes, and technology, and a willingness to embrace change. Here's why organizational readiness is crucial:

1. Efficiency and Effectiveness: An organization that is ready for Problem Management can execute the processes efficiently, leading to quicker problem resolution and minimal disruption to services.

2. Cost Savings: Being prepared for Problem Management allows for better resource allocation, reducing the costs associated with recurring incidents and their impacts.

3. Employee Buy-In: When an organization is ready, employees are more likely to embrace the changes, follow the new processes, and actively contribute to the success of Problem Management.

4. Sustainability: A prepared organization is better positioned to sustain the Problem Management process over time, ensuring long-term benefits.

Now, let's break down the components of organizational readiness for Problem Management and discuss how to assess and improve them.

Key Components of Organizational Readiness

Organizational readiness encompasses several critical components, each of which plays a vital role in ensuring the success of Problem Management:

1. Leadership Support: The commitment and endorsement of organizational leaders are essential for driving the adoption of Problem Management. Leaders should understand its significance and allocate necessary resources.

2. Resource Allocation: Problem Management requires skilled personnel, tools, and financial resources. Adequate resources must be allocated to support the implementation and ongoing operation of Problem Management.

3. Cultural Alignment: The organizational culture should encourage collaboration, continuous improvement, and a proactive approach to problem-solving. Problem Management may require cultural adjustments to ensure buy-in from all stakeholders.

4. Communication and Awareness: Effective communication is key to ensuring that all employees understand the goals, benefits, and processes of Problem Management. Awareness programs and training may be necessary.

5. Technology and Tools: Problem Management relies on technology and tools for efficient problem identification, tracking, and resolution. Ensure that the necessary software and infrastructure are in place.

6. Process Documentation: Problem Management processes should be documented and accessible to all stakeholders. This includes the creation of standard operating procedures and process flows.

7. Metrics and Measurement: Establishing Key Performance Indicators (KPIs) and metrics for Problem Management is vital. The organization should be ready to measure and analyze the effectiveness of the process.

Assessing Organizational Readiness

Before embarking on the implementation of Problem Management, it's crucial to assess your organization's readiness. This assessment helps you identify strengths and weaknesses and guides the development of an action plan for improvement. Here's a step-by-step guide to assessing organizational readiness:

Step 1: Leadership Engagement

Evaluate the level of leadership engagement and support for Problem Management. Consider the following:

- Do senior executives understand the value of Problem Management in improving service quality and reducing costs?
- Are they committed to providing the necessary resources, including budget and personnel, to establish and maintain Problem Management?

Step 2: Resource Assessment

Assess the availability of resources required for Problem Management:

- Do you have staff with the necessary skills and expertise to lead and execute Problem Management processes?
- Are there budgetary provisions for tools, training, and personnel development?
- Does the organization have the physical infrastructure and technology in place to support Problem Management activities?

Step 3: Cultural Alignment

Evaluate the organizational culture and whether it aligns with Problem Management principles:

- Does your organization promote a culture of collaboration and knowledge sharing?
- Is there a history of proactive problem-solving, or does the culture tend to be more reactive in response to incidents?
- Are employees open to change and continuous improvement, or is there resistance to new processes and practices?

Step 4: Communication and Awareness

Assess the level of awareness and understanding of Problem Management:

- Do employees at all levels of the organization understand the goals and benefits of Problem Management?
- Is there a communication plan in place to inform and educate employees about the upcoming changes and the importance of Problem Management?
- Are training and support resources available for employees to acquire the necessary skills and knowledge?

Step 5: Technology and Tools

Evaluate the technology infrastructure and tools available:

- Are there existing IT tools that can be leveraged for Problem Management, or is there a need to invest in dedicated Problem Management software?
- Are these tools integrated with other IT Service Management processes, such as Incident Management and Change Management?

Step 6: Process Documentation

Review the documentation of existing processes and procedures:

- Are Problem Management processes clearly defined, documented, and accessible to relevant personnel?
- Are there standard operating procedures (SOPs) for Problem Management activities?
- Is there a process for updating and maintaining process documentation?

Step 7: Metrics and Measurement

Determine whether the organization has a culture of measuring and improving performance:

- Are there established KPIs and metrics for Problem Management, or is there a need to define and implement these measures?
- Is there a system for collecting, analyzing, and reporting on Problem Management performance data?

Creating an Organizational Readiness Plan

Once you've conducted your assessment, you'll have a clear understanding of your organization's readiness for Problem Management. Now, it's time to create an Organizational Readiness Plan. This plan should outline the specific steps and actions needed to address any gaps in readiness and prepare the organization for the successful implementation of Problem Management.

Here are some key considerations when creating your readiness plan:

1. Leadership Buy-In: If leadership support is lacking, you may need to develop a persuasive case for the importance of Problem Management in achieving organizational goals. This could include showcasing the potential cost savings and improved service quality that can result from effective Problem Management.

2. Resource Planning: Identify resource gaps and create a resource allocation plan. This may involve recruiting or training personnel, acquiring necessary tools, and allocating budgetary resources.

3. Cultural Change: If your organization's culture is not conducive to Problem Management, consider cultural change initiatives. Encourage collaboration, proactive problem-solving, and knowledge sharing through training, communication, and incentive programs.

4. Communication and Training: Develop a comprehensive communication plan that includes awareness programs and training for employees at all levels. Clearly communicate the goals and benefits of Problem Management and ensure that everyone understands their role in its success.

5. Technology Assessment: If technology and tools are lacking, conduct a thorough assessment of the tools and infrastructure needed for Problem Management. Identify suitable software solutions, taking into consideration integration with other IT Service Management processes.

6. Process Documentation: Ensure that Problem Management processes are well-d

ocumented and accessible. Establish a process for regular review and update of documentation to reflect any changes or improvements.

7. Metrics and Measurement: Define a set of KPIs and metrics for Problem Management, and implement the necessary tools and processes to collect, analyze, and report on performance data.

Overcoming Resistance to Change

During the readiness assessment and planning phases, it's not uncommon to encounter resistance to change. Employees and teams may be hesitant to embrace new processes or approaches, fearing disruptions or additional work. Overcoming resistance to change is a critical aspect of ensuring the successful adoption of Problem Management.

Here are some strategies to address and mitigate resistance:

1. Education and Training: Provide clear and comprehensive training on Problem Management principles and processes. Make sure employees understand the benefits of Problem Management and how it will make their work easier, not harder.

2. Engagement and Involvement: Involve employees in the planning and implementation process. Their insights and feedback can be invaluable in refining processes and ensuring they align with practical needs.

3. Communication: Maintain open and transparent communication throughout the implementation process. Address concerns and questions promptly. Regular updates on the progress of Problem Management can help alleviate uncertainty.

4. Demonstrate Success: As you begin to implement Problem Management, share success stories and achievements. This can help build enthusiasm and confidence in the process.

5. Incentives: Consider providing incentives for employees who actively engage with Problem Management and contribute to its success. Recognize and reward those who excel in problem-solving and proactive measures.

Organizational readiness is the foundation upon which effective Problem Management is built. By conducting a thorough assessment, identifying areas for improvement, and creating an Organizational Readiness Plan, you can pave the way for a successful implementation. Remember that change can be met with resistance, so it's essential to engage and communicate with employees throughout the process. In the following chapters, we'll delve deeper into the specific steps for defining Problem Management processes, assembling a Problem Management team, identifying key stakeholders, and creating policies to guide your efforts. These are all essential components of a comprehensive Problem Management framework that is ready to meet the challenges of the IT environment.

Defining Problem Management Processes

The success of Problem Management hinges on the clarity and precision of its processes. In this chapter, we will explore the critical steps involved in defining Problem Management processes. From problem identification to resolution, creating a well-structured and efficient process is key to achieving the goals of Problem Management and improving IT service quality.

The Anatomy of Problem Management Processes

Problem Management is a structured and systematic approach to identifying, documenting, and resolving underlying causes of incidents. The processes within Problem Management are designed to manage problems from their detection through to resolution, and subsequently, prevention. Here is an overview of the key processes involved in Problem Management:

1. Problem Identification and Logging: The process begins with the identification of problems, often initiated by incident data. Once identified, these problems are formally logged and documented in a problem record.

2. Problem Categorization and Prioritization: The next step involves categorizing and prioritizing problems based on factors like impact, urgency, and business relevance. Categorization helps in efficiently assigning resources and addressing the most critical issues first.

3. Investigation and Diagnosis: This process is at the core of Problem Management. It involves the investigation of the problem, root cause analysis, and the development of a permanent solution. It's the step where the problem-solving journey truly begins.

4. Resolution and Workarounds: Problems are resolved by implementing permanent solutions. Meanwhile, temporary workarounds might be employed to minimize the impact of the problem on service delivery.

5. Incident and Problem Relationship: Establishing the link between incidents and problems is crucial. This process ensures that recurring incidents stemming from the same problem are addressed through Problem Management.

6. Knowledge Management: A robust knowledge management process is essential for capturing, storing, and sharing knowledge related to problems and their solutions. It supports continuous improvement.

7. Metrics and Reporting: Problem Management processes are monitored and measured using key performance indicators (KPIs) and metrics. Reporting on these metrics helps in assessing the efficiency and effectiveness of Problem Management.

Defining Problem Management Processes

Now, let's delve into the process of defining these Problem Management processes to ensure that they are tailored to your organization's specific needs.

1. Problem Identification and Logging

Step 1: Problem Identification

- Problem identification typically begins with the detection of recurring incidents or patterns of incidents. This can be achieved through data analysis, incident records, feedback from end-users, or monitoring tools.

- Establish a clear process for the identification of problems. Make sure all incidents are reviewed, and patterns are recognized.

Step 2: Problem Logging

- Once a potential problem is identified, it needs to be formally logged. This involves creating a problem record, which contains detailed information about the problem, including its description, date of identification, and initial impact assessment.

- Implement standardized templates for problem records. This ensures that essential information is consistently captured for each problem.

2. Problem Categorization and Prioritization

Step 1: Categorization

- After a problem is logged, it should be categorized based on predefined criteria. Categories can include technology type, affected services, and severity of the problem.

- Develop a problem categorization schema that aligns with your organization's service portfolio. Ensure that all relevant categories are defined.

Step 2: Prioritization

- Problems must be prioritized based on their impact, urgency, and business significance. This step determines the order in which problems will be addressed.

- Define clear criteria for prioritization, such as the potential impact on service availability, the number of incidents related to the problem, and the criticality of affected business processes.

3. Investigation and Diagnosis

Step 1: Problem Investigation

- The heart of Problem Management lies in investigating problems thoroughly. This step involves the creation of a problem investigation team or assigning the problem to a qualified individual.

- Clearly define roles and responsibilities within the problem investigation team. Ensure that team members have the necessary skills and tools for analysis.

Step 2: Root Cause Analysis

- Root cause analysis is a critical part of Problem Management. It involves systematically identifying the underlying reasons for the problem. Various techniques, such as the "5 Whys" or Fishbone diagrams, can be used.

- Establish a standard methodology for root cause analysis that is consistently applied to all problems. Encourage collaboration and brainstorming within the investigation team.

Step 3: Permanent Solution Development

- Once the root cause is identified, the next step is to develop a permanent solution to prevent the problem from recurring. This may involve changes to technology, processes, or policies.

- Ensure that changes to the IT environment are managed through Change Management processes. This helps avoid introducing new issues while addressing the problem.

4. Resolution and Workarounds

Step 1: Problem Resolution

- Problem resolution is the implementation of the permanent solution. This step should result in the elimination of the problem's root cause.

- Coordinate with Change Management to plan, test, and implement the necessary changes to resolve the problem. Ensure that changes are communicated to affected parties.

Step 2: Workarounds

- In some cases, it may be necessary to implement temporary workarounds to mitigate the impact of the problem while the permanent solution is being developed and implemented.

- Develop a process for documenting and communicating workarounds. Ensure that workarounds are clearly documented in problem records.

5. Incident and Problem Relationship

Step 1: Linking Incidents and Problems

- The relationship between incidents and problems is essential for efficient Problem Management. It ensures that recurring incidents are addressed through the Problem Management process.

- Implement a process for linking incidents to problems. Ensure that the Incident Management process provides a means to identify and link incidents that are part of the same problem.

Step 2: Incident Resolution

- As problems are resolved, related incidents should be updated to reflect the resolution and to close the incidents. This step should ensure that affected services return to normal operation.

- Establish clear communication channels between Problem Management and Incident Management to update and close related incidents promptly.

6. Knowledge Management in Problem Management

Step 1: Knowledge Capture and Storage

- Capturing knowledge related to problems and their solutions is a fundamental aspect of Problem Management. Establish a knowledge base where this information is stored and easily accessible.

- Select appropriate knowledge management tools and platforms to capture and manage knowledge. Ensure that the knowledge base is searchable and well-organized.

Step 2: Knowledge Sharing and Transfer

- Knowledge sharing within the Problem Management team and across the organization is critical. This step ensures that lessons learned are applied to prevent future problems.

- Create a process for sharing knowledge within the team and organization. Encourage the documentation of best practices and solutions.

7. Metrics and Reporting

Step 1: Define Key Performance Indicators (KPIs)

- KPIs are essential for measuring the effectiveness of Problem Management. Define KPIs that align with your organization's goals and objectives.

- Common KPIs include the mean time to resolve problems, the number of recurring incidents, and the percentage of problems resolved within target timelines.

Step 2: Data Collection and Analysis

- Implement mechanisms for collecting and analyzing data related to Problem Management processes and their outcomes. This data provides insights into the efficiency and effectiveness of the processes.

- Use reporting tools and data analysis techniques to derive actionable insights from the collected data.

Step 3: Continuous Improvement

- Problem Management is an iterative

 process. Regularly review the results of your Problem Management processes and identify areas for improvement.

- Use data and feedback to drive continuous improvement in the Problem Management processes. Encourage a culture of learning and adaptability.

Customizing Problem Management Processes

It's important to note that while the fundamental structure of Problem Management processes remains consistent, each organization may need to customize these processes to align with its unique requirements, industry, and scale of operations. Customization can involve tailoring processes to meet specific regulatory requirements, the complexity of IT services, and the size and structure of the organization.

Customization considerations include:

- Regulatory Compliance: Ensure that your Problem Management processes comply with industry-specific regulations and standards. For example, healthcare organizations may have specific requirements related to the handling of patient data.

- Service Complexity: Organizations offering a wide range of services may need more detailed problem categorization and prioritization processes to handle a variety of service types.

- Organization Size: Smaller organizations may have simpler Problem Management processes due to reduced scale, while larger enterprises may require more complex and scalable processes.

- Industry Focus: Some industries have specific needs, such as financial organizations requiring additional layers of approval and documentation due to compliance and security concerns.

- Integration with Other ITIL Processes: Ensure that Problem Management processes are integrated with other ITIL processes, such as Incident Management, Change Management, and Service Level Management.

Conclusion

Defining Problem Management processes is a critical step in establishing a robust and effective framework for addressing IT problems and preventing incidents. These processes ensure that problems are systematically identified, analyzed, and resolved, leading to improved service quality and reduced operational costs. By customizing these processes to suit your organization's unique requirements and continually measuring and improving their efficiency, you can derive the maximum benefit from Problem Management. In the following chapters, we will explore other essential aspects of Problem Management, including assembling a Problem Management team, identifying key stakeholders, creating policies, and setting up automation tools to support your Problem Management processes.

Building a Problem Management Team

A successful Problem Management process requires a dedicated and skilled team that can systematically identify, analyze, and resolve problems. This chapter delves into the intricacies of building a Problem Management team, focusing on assembling the right individuals, defining their roles and responsibilities, and fostering a collaborative and proactive work environment.

The Importance of a Skilled Problem Management Team

Your Problem Management team is the engine that drives the entire process. The team's composition and competence are crucial for the effectiveness of Problem Management. Here's why the team is so important:

1. Expertise: A skilled team possesses the knowledge and expertise required for in-depth problem analysis and effective root cause identification.

2. Efficiency: The right team can efficiently manage problems, reduce the mean time to resolution (MTTR), and minimize the impact of incidents on your organization.

3. Proactivity: A proactive team can anticipate and prevent problems from recurring, ensuring a more stable and reliable IT environment.

4. Collaboration: Effective collaboration within the team and with other ITIL processes, such as Incident Management and Change Management, is vital for Problem Management success.

Building the Problem Management Team

Building a Problem Management team involves several key steps. These steps are crucial for ensuring that your team is well-structured, properly trained, and aligned with your organization's goals.

Step 1: Define Roles and Responsibilities

Before you start assembling your Problem Management team, it's important to define the roles and responsibilities within the team. This includes:

- Problem Manager: The Problem Manager is responsible for overseeing the Problem Management process, ensuring that problems are properly identified, investigated, and resolved. They coordinate the team's activities and serve as the main point of contact for senior management.

- Problem Analysts: Problem Analysts are responsible for investigating and analyzing problems, identifying root causes, and developing permanent solutions. They work closely with other teams, such as Incident Management, to gather information and investigate incidents associated with problems.

- Problem Coordinators: Problem Coordinators play a critical role in managing the day-to-day activities of Problem Management. They ensure that problems are properly logged, categorized, and prioritized. They may also assist in coordinating resources for investigations.

- Knowledge Managers: Knowledge Managers focus on capturing, storing, and sharing knowledge related to problems and their solutions. They maintain the knowledge base and ensure that valuable insights are shared within the team and across the organization.

- Change Management Liaison: The Change Management Liaison acts as a bridge between Problem Management and Change Management. They ensure that changes required to address problems are properly evaluated and approved.

Step 2: Assemble the Team

Once you have defined the roles and responsibilities, it's time to assemble your Problem Management team. Depending on the size and complexity of your organization, you may have a small or large team. Key considerations include:

- Skills and Expertise: Ensure that team members possess the necessary skills and expertise. Problem Analysts, for instance, should have strong analytical and investigative skills.

- Cross-Functional Knowledge: Encourage diversity in the team, with members who have knowledge of various aspects of IT, including hardware, software, and networks.

- Training: Invest in training and development for team members to keep their skills up to date and aligned with industry best practices.

- Collaboration: Select team members who are willing to collaborate and share information with other teams, as Problem Management often involves coordination with Incident Management, Change Management, and other ITIL processes.

Step 3: Training and Development

A well-trained team is crucial for the success of Problem Management. The following considerations are essential for training and development:

- ITIL Training: Ensure that team members receive training in ITIL principles and Problem Management practices. ITIL certifications, such as ITIL Foundation or ITIL Practitioner, can be valuable.

- Technical Training: Invest in technical training to keep team members updated on the latest technologies and tools relevant to Problem Management.

- Soft Skills: Problem Analysts should have strong analytical and communication skills to effectively investigate and document problems.

- Continuous Learning: Encourage team members to engage in continuous learning and stay updated on industry trends and best practices.

Step 4: Foster a Collaborative Environment

Collaboration is essential within the Problem Management team and with other ITIL processes. Here's how to foster a collaborative environment:

- Regular Meetings: Conduct regular team meetings to discuss ongoing investigations, share insights, and plan problem resolution activities.

- Information Sharing: Promote an open culture of information sharing. Encourage team members to share their findings and knowledge with the team and the wider organization.

- Communication Channels: Establish clear communication channels between Problem Management and other ITIL processes, such as Incident Management, to facilitate the exchange of information.

- Problem Review Boards: Consider setting up a Problem Review Board that includes representatives from various IT teams. This board can review and approve the implementation of permanent solutions.

Step 5: Leadership and Coordination

Effective leadership and coordination are crucial for guiding the team and ensuring that Problem Management processes run smoothly:

- Problem Manager's Role: The Problem Manager plays a pivotal role in overseeing the team and the entire Problem Management process. They provide leadership, set priorities, and coordinate the team's activities.

- Change Management Coordination: Ensure that the Change Management Liaison effectively coordinates with the Change Management process. This coordination is essential for evaluating and approving changes that are required to address problems.

- Resource Allocation: Coordinate the allocation of resources for problem investigations, ensuring that the team has the necessary tools and personnel to execute their tasks.

Step 6: Escalation and Communication

Define escalation procedures for problems that require senior management attention or specialized expertise. Establish a clear process for communication between the Problem Management team and senior management. Ensure that senior management is informed of the progress and impact of Problem Management efforts.

Step 7: Documenting and Reporting

Create a clear process for documenting the team's activities and problem investigations. Ensure that problem records are well-maintained and that findings and solutions are properly documented. Develop reporting mechanisms to communicate the team's progress and results to senior management and other stakeholders.

Measuring Team Performance

To ensure that your Problem Management team is effective, it's important to establish key performance indicators (KPIs) and metrics that measure the team's performance. These metrics can include:

- Mean Time to Resolve (MTTR) Problems: This metric measures the average time it takes to resolve problems, reflecting the team's efficiency.

- Number of Recurring Incidents: A decrease in the number of incidents related to the same problem is a sign of successful problem resolution.

- Percentage of Problems Resolved: This metric measures the success rate in resolving problems within target timelines.

- Customer Satisfaction: Collect feedback from end-users and stakeholders to gauge their satisfaction with the Problem Management process.

- Knowledge Base Utilization: Measure how frequently the knowledge base is accessed and updated by team members and other IT staff.

A skilled and well-organized Problem Management team is essential for effectively identifying, analyzing, and resolving IT problems. The team's expertise, collaboration, and dedication are key to reducing the mean time to resolution, minimizing incident impact, and ensuring a more stable and reliable IT environment. By defining roles and responsibilities, assembling the right team, providing training and development, fostering a collaborative environment, and measuring, you can build a high-performing Problem Management team that contributes to the success of your IT Service Management framework

Identifying Key Stakeholders in Problem Management

Effective Problem Management doesn't happen in isolation. It relies on the active involvement and cooperation of various stakeholders within your organization. In this chapter, we'll explore the critical step of identifying key stakeholders in Problem Management and understanding their roles and responsibilities. This essential task ensures that the Problem Management process aligns with the needs and goals of the organization as a whole.

Why Identifying Key Stakeholders Matters

Stakeholders are individuals or groups who have a vested interest in the outcome of Problem Management activities. Their engagement is crucial for several reasons:

1. Support and Resources: Key stakeholders provide the necessary support, resources, and budget required to establish and sustain Problem Management processes.

2. Alignment with Organizational Goals: Understanding the needs and priorities of stakeholders helps ensure that Problem Management activities are in line with the organization's strategic objectives.

3. Information Sharing: Effective communication with stakeholders ensures that they are informed about the progress and results of Problem Management efforts.

4. Issue Resolution: Stakeholders can play a role in resolving issues and challenges that may arise during Problem Management activities.

5. Continuous Improvement: Stakeholder feedback can contribute to the continuous improvement of Problem Management processes and their alignment with the changing needs of the organization.

Identifying Key Stakeholders

The process of identifying key stakeholders involves a systematic approach to mapping out the individuals and groups that have an interest in or impact on Problem Management. Here's how to get started:

1. Internal Stakeholders

IT Leadership:
- Chief Information Officer (CIO): The CIO may provide high-level support and resources for Problem Management, aligning it with the organization's strategic goals.
- IT Directors/Managers: IT directors and managers are responsible for overseeing IT operations and ensuring that Problem Management is integrated into the overall IT Service Management framework.

- IT Service Owners: Service owners have a vested interest in Problem Management, as it directly affects the quality and reliability of their respective services.

Problem Management Team:
- Problem Manager: The Problem Manager is a key internal stakeholder responsible for driving Problem Management activities and ensuring the team's needs are met.
- Problem Analysts: Problem Analysts actively engage in problem investigations and root cause analysis, making their input valuable.

Incident Management Team:
- Collaboration with Incident Management is crucial, as incidents often lead to the identification of problems.

Change Management Team:
- Change Management is closely related to Problem Management, as permanent solutions often involve changes to the IT environment.

Knowledge Management Team:
- The Knowledge Management team is responsible for capturing and sharing knowledge related to problems and their solutions.

Service Desk/Support Teams:
- Service desk and support teams handle incidents on a daily basis. Their feedback can help identify recurring problems and improve Problem Management processes.

2. External Stakeholders

Vendors and Suppliers:
- Vendors and suppliers of IT services or components are stakeholders if their products or services are part of the IT environment. Their cooperation may be necessary for problem resolution.

Regulatory Bodies:
- If your organization is subject to industry-specific regulations, regulatory bodies may be external stakeholders with a vested interest in Problem Management compliance.

3. End-Users and Customers

While not directly involved in the technical aspects of Problem Management, end-users and customers are critical stakeholders. Their satisfaction is closely tied to the effectiveness of Problem Management in preventing incidents and minimizing disruptions to services.

4. Business and Operations Units

Various business and operations units within your organization may also be considered stakeholders. Their concerns can include the impact of IT problems on business processes and customer service. Understanding their needs and priorities is essential for effective Problem Management.

Engaging Key Stakeholders

Once key stakeholders are identified, the next step is to engage them in the Problem Management process. Here are some key strategies for stakeholder engagement:

1. Communication Plans:
- Develop clear communication plans that outline how and when stakeholders will be informed about Problem Management activities, progress, and outcomes.

2. Regular Meetings:
- Schedule regular meetings with key stakeholders to discuss problem investigations, solutions, and overall progress.

3. Feedback Mechanisms:
- Provide channels for stakeholders to provide feedback and raise concerns. Encourage open and honest dialogue.

4. Involvement in Decision-Making:
- Include stakeholders in decision-making processes related to Problem Management activities, such as prioritizing problems and approving changes.

5. Education and Training:
- Ensure that stakeholders have a basic understanding of Problem Management processes and their role in them. This can be achieved through training and educational materials.

6. Support and Resources:
- Clearly communicate the support and resources required from stakeholders to facilitate Problem Management processes.

7. Reporting and Metrics:
- Share relevant data and metrics with stakeholders to demonstrate the impact and value of Problem Management efforts.

8. Issue Resolution:
- Establish a process for addressing issues and concerns raised by stakeholders promptly.

Continuous Improvement through Stakeholder Feedback

Stakeholder feedback is a valuable source of insights for the continuous improvement of Problem Management processes. Here's how to leverage stakeholder feedback:

1. Regular Surveys:
- Conduct regular surveys to gather feedback from stakeholders. Ask about their satisfaction with Problem Management activities and identify areas for improvement.

2. Review Meetings:
- Hold review meetings with stakeholders to discuss their concerns, suggestions, and expectations. Use these insights to make necessary adjustments to Problem Management processes.

3. Incorporate Feedback:
- Act on the feedback received from stakeholders to improve Problem Management processes, communication, and overall effectiveness.

4. Benchmarking:
- Compare your organization's Problem Management practices with industry benchmarks and best practices. Use this information to align with stakeholder expectations and industry standards.

Identifying key stakeholders is a crucial step in ensuring the success of your Problem Management process. Engaging stakeholders from both within and outside the organization, and understanding their needs, priorities, and expectations, is essential for effective problem identification, analysis, and resolution. By fostering collaboration, communication, and feedback with key stakeholders, your organization can leverage their support and resources to drive the continuous improvement of Problem Management practices.

Creating a Problem Management Policy

A Problem Management policy is the foundation upon which an effective Problem Management framework is built. It provides the guidelines, objectives, and responsibilities for managing problems in the IT environment. In this chapter, we will explore the key components and considerations involved in creating a Problem Management policy.

The Importance of a Problem Management Policy

A well-defined Problem Management policy serves as a critical reference point for the entire organization. It is the roadmap that outlines how problems are identified, analyzed, and resolved. Here's why a Problem Management policy is essential:

1. Standardization: It sets standard procedures and practices for handling problems, ensuring consistency and reliability in problem resolution.

2. Alignment with Goals: The policy aligns Problem Management activities with the strategic goals and objectives of the organization.

3. Responsibility: It assigns clear responsibilities to individuals and teams, creating accountability for problem resolution.

4. Communication: The policy facilitates communication by defining the roles and responsibilities of different stakeholders and their involvement in Problem Management.

5. Continuous Improvement: It provides a framework for ongoing review and optimization of Problem Management processes, leading to increased efficiency.

Creating a Problem Management Policy

Creating a Problem Management policy involves several key steps and considerations. Let's explore these in detail:

Step 1: Define Policy Objectives

Begin by defining the objectives of your Problem Management policy. What do you aim to achieve with Problem Management? Consider objectives such as:

- Reducing the mean time to resolve (MTTR) problems.
- Minimizing the impact of incidents on service quality.
- Preventing the recurrence of problems.
- Enhancing the overall quality of IT services.
- Increasing customer and end-user satisfaction.

The objectives you set should align with the strategic goals of your organization and reflect the desired outcomes of Problem Management.

Step 2: Identify Stakeholder Roles and Responsibilities

Clearly define the roles and responsibilities of key stakeholders involved in Problem Management. This includes roles such as:

- Problem Manager
- Problem Analysts
- Problem Coordinators
- Change Management Liaison
- Knowledge Managers
- Service Desk/Support Teams

For each role, specify their responsibilities, authority, and accountability. It's important that everyone involved understands their role in the Problem Management process.

Step 3: Define Problem Management Processes

Your policy should outline the Problem Management processes, including:

- Problem Identification and Logging
- Problem Categorization and Prioritization
- Investigation and Diagnosis
- Resolution and Workarounds

- Incident and Problem Relationship
- Knowledge Management
- Metrics and Reporting

Each process should be described in sufficient detail to ensure that everyone involved understands the steps involved and their place in the overall framework.

Step 4: Establish Process Flows

Create process flows that visually represent the sequence of activities for each Problem Management process. These process flows provide a clear, step-by-step guide for executing Problem Management activities. Make sure to include any dependencies or interactions with other ITIL processes, such as Incident Management and Change Management.

Step 5: Set Quality Standards

Define the quality standards and performance metrics that will be used to measure the effectiveness of Problem Management. Common metrics include:

- Mean Time to Resolve (MTTR) Problems
- Number of Recurring Incidents
- Percentage of Problems Resolved within Target Timelines
- Customer and End-User Satisfaction

By setting quality standards, you provide a benchmark for assessing the success of your Problem Management efforts.

Step 6: Establish Reporting and Communication Procedures

Your policy should outline the reporting and communication procedures for Problem Management. Define who needs to be informed about problem investigations, progress, and outcomes. Consider the following:

- Regular reports to senior management on Problem Management performance and impact.
- Communication channels between Problem Management and other ITIL processes, such as Change Management.
- Procedures for updating and sharing knowledge related to problems and solutions.

Step 7: Incorporate Regulatory and Compliance Requirements

If your organization is subject to industry-specific regulations or standards, ensure that your Problem Management policy incorporates the necessary requirements. This may involve additional documentation, reporting, or procedures to ensure compliance.

Step 8: Document Escalation Procedures

Define clear escalation procedures for problems that require senior management attention or specialized expertise. Include criteria for escalating problems and specify the responsible parties at each level of escalation.

Step 9: Document Roles in Incident and Problem Relationship

Clearly define the relationship between Incident Management and Problem Management in your policy. Describe the roles and responsibilities of both teams in identifying, linking, and resolving incidents related to problems.

Step 10: Include Change Management Integration

Outline the integration between Change Management and Problem Management. Describe how changes required to address problems are evaluated, approved, and implemented within the Change Management process.

Step 11: Address Continuous Improvement

Highlight the importance of continuous improvement within Problem Management. Encourage the team to review and optimize processes and practices regularly. Define a process for capturing and implementing lessons learned.

Step 12: Review and Approval

Before finalizing your Problem Management policy, it should go through a review and approval process. Key stakeholders and senior management should review the policy for alignment with organizational objectives and compliance with regulations. Once approved, the policy can be implemented.

Step 13: Training and Education

Ensure that all relevant staff members are trained and educated on the Problem Management policy. This includes team members, incident handlers, and anyone who plays a role in problem identification and resolution.

Customization Considerations

It's important to customize your Problem Management policy to suit your organization's unique needs and requirements. Consider the following customization factors:

- Industry Focus: Some industries, such as healthcare or finance, may have specific regulatory or security requirements that need to be incorporated into the policy

.

- Service Complexity: Customize the policy to align with the complexity of your IT services. For organizations with a wide range of services, more detailed processes and documentation may be necessary.

- Organization Size: Smaller organizations may have simpler Problem Management policies, while larger enterprises may require more complex and scalable policies.

- Integration with Other ITIL Processes: Ensure that the policy is integrated with other ITIL processes, such as Incident Management, Change Management, and Service Level Management.

Continuous Review and Updates

A Problem Management policy is not a static document. It should be subject to regular review and updates to ensure that it remains relevant and effective. Key elements of the policy may need to be revised in response to changing organizational goals, regulatory requirements, or industry best practices.

Creating a Problem Management policy is a critical step in establishing a structured and effective framework for managing IT problems. The policy provides the foundation for problem identification, analysis, and resolution and ensures that Problem Management activities are aligned with the goals and objectives of your organization. By customizing the policy to suit your organization's unique needs and continually reviewing and updating it, you can ensure that Problem Management remains a vital component of your IT Service Management framework.

Detecting Problems

Detecting problems in the IT environment is a foundational step in the Problem Management process. It involves identifying underlying issues that are causing recurring incidents and service disruptions. In this chapter, we will explore the methods, tools, and best practices for effectively detecting problems in your IT infrastructure.

The Significance of Problem Detection

Problem detection is the proactive process of identifying and addressing the root causes of incidents. This process is vital for several reasons:

1. Minimizing Disruptions: By detecting problems early, you can prevent recurring incidents and reduce the overall impact on IT services and end-users.

2. Cost Reduction: Timely problem detection helps in managing and controlling costs by preventing the escalation of issues and the need for extensive incident resolution efforts.

3. Improved Service Quality: Addressing underlying problems leads to increased service reliability and quality, enhancing end-user satisfaction.

4. Supporting ITIL Processes: Problem detection is essential for Incident Management, Change Management, and other ITIL processes as it provides valuable insights into recurring issues and required changes.

Methods for Problem Detection

Effective problem detection requires a systematic and proactive approach. Here are some key methods and best practices for identifying problems in your IT environment:

1. Incident Data Analysis:

- One of the primary sources for problem detection is incident data. Analyzing incident records can reveal patterns and recurring issues that are indicative of underlying problems.

- Develop a robust incident categorization and coding system to help identify commonalities among incidents. This system can help you identify problem trends.

2. Trend Analysis:

- Trend analysis involves monitoring patterns of incidents over time. It helps in identifying recurring incidents and discerning whether they are part of a broader problem.

- Use statistical and data analysis tools to detect significant trends in incident data.

3. Root Cause Analysis (RCA):

- Root cause analysis is a structured method for identifying the underlying causes of incidents and problems. It involves techniques such as the "5 Whys" and Fishbone diagrams to trace issues back to their origins.

- Invest in training your team in RCA techniques, and integrate RCA into your problem detection process.

4. Change Impact Analysis:

- Changes to the IT environment can introduce new problems or exacerbate existing ones. Conduct change impact analysis to identify problems that may be linked to recent changes.

- Collaborate closely with the Change Management process to ensure that changes are thoroughly assessed for potential problem impacts.

5. User Feedback:

- End-users can provide valuable feedback on recurring issues they encounter. Establish a feedback mechanism that allows users to report problems, and use this feedback as a source for problem detection.

- Implement a user-friendly service desk portal or ticketing system for issue reporting.

6. Monitoring and Alerting:

- Proactive monitoring of IT systems and infrastructure can help detect issues before they impact end-users. Monitoring tools can generate alerts for conditions that may lead to problems.

- Implement robust monitoring solutions that cover critical components of your IT environment.

7. Collaboration with Incident Management:

- Close collaboration with the Incident Management process is essential for problem detection. Incident handlers should be trained to identify patterns and recurring issues that may indicate problems.

- Create a clear process for escalating incidents to problem investigations when a potential problem is identified.

Tools for Problem Detection

The use of appropriate tools can significantly enhance problem detection efforts. Here are some tools commonly used in problem detection:

1. Incident Management Software:

- Incident management software helps in capturing and tracking incidents. It can provide data and reports that aid in problem detection.

2. Monitoring and Alerting Tools:

- Monitoring tools, such as Nagios, Zabbix, and SolarWinds, can help in identifying abnormal system behavior and generating alerts when predefined thresholds are exceeded.

3. RCA Tools:

- Root cause analysis tools, such as Fishbone diagrams and Pareto charts, can assist in identifying the root causes of recurring incidents.

4. Data Analysis and Reporting Tools:

- Data analysis and reporting tools, such as Tableau or Power BI, can be used to analyze incident data and generate reports that highlight recurring issues.

5. Feedback and Service Desk Software:

- Feedback and service desk software, like ServiceNow or Jira Service Desk, can capture end-user feedback and incidents, which can be valuable for problem detection.

Best Practices for Effective Problem Detection

Effective problem detection requires a systematic approach and adherence to best practices. Here are some best practices to enhance your problem detection process:

1. Establish a Clear Detection Process:

- Define a step-by-step process for problem detection, including data analysis, trend analysis, incident categorization, and RCA.

2. Continuous Monitoring:

- Implement continuous monitoring of your IT environment to identify potential problems as soon as they arise.

3. Incident Categorization:

- Develop a robust system for categorizing and coding incidents. This system should help in identifying patterns and trends.

4. Incident Ownership:

- Assign ownership to incidents, and ensure that incident handlers understand their role in problem detection and escalation.

5. RCA Integration:

- Integrate root cause analysis into your problem detection process. Whenever a significant incident occurs, perform RCA to identify underlying problems.

6. Collaboration with Other ITIL Processes:

- Collaborate closely with Incident Management and Change Management processes to ensure that problem detection is well-integrated.

7. User Feedback Channels:

- Provide clear channels for end-users to report issues and provide feedback. Act on this feedback to detect potential problems.

8. Knowledge Sharing:

- Encourage knowledge sharing within the team. Ensure that incident handlers and problem analysts share insights and information that may help detect problems.

9. Data Analysis Training:

- Train your team in data analysis techniques to help them identify trends and patterns in incident data.

10. Incident History Review:

- Regularly review the incident history to identify incidents that are indicative of problems. Conduct reviews at defined intervals.

11. Continuous Improvement:

- As you detect and resolve

 problems, use the knowledge gained to improve your problem detection process continuously.

Effective problem detection is a critical component of Problem Management. It helps in identifying the root causes of recurring incidents and service disruptions, ultimately leading to improved service quality and customer satisfaction. By following systematic methods, using appropriate tools, and adhering to best practices, your organization can establish a robust problem detection process.

Logging Problem Records

Logging problem records is a foundational step in the Problem Management process. Problem records serve as the documentation that captures essential information about identified problems, enabling efficient analysis and resolution. In this chapter, we will explore the significance of logging problem records, the key components of problem records, and best practices for effective logging.

The Importance of Logging Problem Records

Problem records are the backbone of Problem Management. They play a vital role for several reasons:

1. Documentation: Problem records provide a structured way to document information about identified problems. This documentation is crucial for analysis, resolution, and reporting.

2. Tracking Progress: They help in tracking the progress of problem investigations and resolution efforts. Problem records serve as a historical record of the problem's lifecycle.

3. Communication: Problem records facilitate effective communication within the Problem Management team and with other stakeholders, such as Incident Management and Change Management.

4. Data Analysis: They serve as a source of data for analyzing trends and patterns in recurring incidents and problems. This data is invaluable for root cause analysis.

Key Components of a Problem Record

A well-structured problem record contains several key components that provide a comprehensive view of the problem. These components include:

1. Problem Identifier:
   - A unique identifier for the problem record, which is used for tracking and referencing.

2. Problem Description:
   - A clear and concise description of the problem, including its symptoms, impact on services, and any relevant details.

3. Date and Time of Detection:
   - The date and time when the problem was initially detected or reported.

4. Incident References:
   - References to incidents that are related to the problem. This linkage helps in understanding the incidents that led to problem detection.

5. Problem Categorization:
   - The problem's categorization and classification, which helps in organizing and prioritizing problems.

6. Problem Priority:
   - The priority level assigned to the problem, indicating its impact and urgency.

7. Problem Owner:
   - The individual or team responsible for managing and resolving the problem.

8. Initial Analysis:
   - A summary of the initial analysis of the problem, including potential causes and impacts.

9. Affected Services:
   - A list of IT services and components that are impacted by the problem.

10. Incident Trends:
   - A summary of incident trends related to the problem, showing how often the problem has led to incidents.

11. Previous Problem Records:
   - References to any previous problem records related to the same underlying issue.

12. Escalation Points:
   - Defined points of escalation within the problem management process for cases where additional expertise or resources are required.

13. Change Requirements:
   - Any identified changes or updates required to resolve the problem, which should be linked to the Change Management process.

Best Practices for Logging Problem Records

To ensure effective problem logging, consider the following best practices:

1. Standardized Templates:
   - Create standardized problem record templates that capture all essential components. This ensures consistency in documentation.

2. Clear Descriptions:
   - Ensure that problem descriptions are clear, concise, and provide a comprehensive understanding of the problem's impact and symptoms.

3. Timely Logging:
   - Log problem records as soon as a problem is detected or reported. Timely logging is essential for tracking and resolution.

4. Categorization and Prioritization:
   - Use a consistent categorization and prioritization system to classify problems. This system helps in organizing and addressing problems based on their urgency and impact.

5. Problem Owner Assignment:
   - Assign a responsible problem owner to each problem record. The problem owner is accountable for the problem's resolution.

6. Incident References:
   - Clearly reference related incidents within the problem record to establish the link between incidents and the underlying problem.

7. Continuous Updates:
   - Continuously update problem records with new information, findings, and progress. This keeps all stakeholders informed.

8. Incident Trends Analysis:
   - Regularly analyze incident trends associated with the problem. This analysis can help in understanding the scope and impact of the problem.

9. Escalation Points:
   - Define and document clear escalation points within the problem record for cases where the problem's resolution requires additional expertise or resources.

10. Change Requirements:
    - Identify and document any required changes or updates that are necessary to resolve the problem. Ensure that these are linked to the Change Management process.

11. Collaboration with Incident Management:
    - Collaborate closely with the Incident Management process to ensure that problem records are generated when incidents indicate a recurring issue.

12. Periodic Review:

- Periodically review problem records to assess progress and make adjustments to the problem management process.

Documentation Tools and Software

To facilitate problem record logging, organizations often use dedicated software and tools. Some popular choices include:

- ServiceNow: ServiceNow offers a comprehensive IT Service Management (ITSM) platform that includes problem management capabilities and problem record logging.

- Jira Service Desk: Jira Service Desk by Atlassian is a versatile service management platform that can be customized to accommodate problem record logging.

- BMC Remedy: BMC Remedy is a widely used IT service management and help desk software that includes problem management features.

- Zendesk: Zendesk is a customer service and engagement platform that can be configured for IT service management, including problem record logging.

- Custom Database Systems: Some organizations create custom databases or use existing relational database management systems (RDBMS) to log and manage problem records.

The choice of tool should align with your organization's needs, budget, and existing IT service management infrastructure.

Logging problem records is a fundamental step in the Problem Management process. Problem records serve as the foundation for tracking, analyzing, and resolving problems, and they facilitate communication within the Problem Management team and with other stakeholders. By following best practices and using standardized templates, you can ensure that problem records provide a comprehensive and structured view of identified problems.

Categorizing Problems

Categorizing problems is an essential step in Problem Management that allows for organized and structured handling of issues within your IT environment. By classifying problems into distinct categories, you can prioritize, investigate, and resolve them more effectively. In this chapter, we will delve into the significance of categorizing problems, the key considerations, and best practices for this process.

The Significance of Problem Categorization

Problem categorization is crucial for the following reasons:

- Prioritization: Categorizing problems enables you to assign priority levels based on their impact and urgency. This ensures that the most critical problems are addressed first.

- Efficient Resource Allocation: It helps in allocating resources more efficiently, as each problem category may require specific expertise or tools.

- Effective Trend Analysis: Categorization aids in the identification of recurring issues and trends, making it easier to identify root causes and implement long-term solutions.

- Communication: Clear categories simplify communication between team members and stakeholders, ensuring that everyone understands the nature and scope of a problem.

Key Considerations for Problem Categorization

To effectively categorize problems, consider the following key considerations:

1. Classification Criteria:
   - Establish clear criteria for classifying problems. Criteria may include the nature of the problem, the services affected, or the potential impact on the organization.

2. Category Definitions:
   - Define categories and subcategories that align with your organization's specific needs and services. These definitions should be consistent and understood by the Problem Management team.

3. Priority Levels:
   - Assign priority levels to each problem category based on the severity of the issue and its impact on services and operations.

4. Escalation Points:
   - Define escalation points for each category, specifying when and how issues should be escalated to higher levels of expertise or management.

5. Documentation:
   - Document the categorization process and criteria in your Problem Management policy and guidelines to ensure consistency and transparency.

6. Training:
   - Ensure that the Problem Management team is trained and familiar with the categorization criteria and process.

Best Practices for Problem Categorization

To optimize problem categorization, follow these best practices:

1. Standardized Categories:

- Use a standardized set of categories and subcategories to ensure consistency and clarity in the categorization process.

2. Clear Definitions:
   - Provide clear and concise definitions for each category, including examples to help team members understand how to apply them.

3. Regular Review:
   - Periodically review and update problem categories to adapt to changing circumstances and technologies.

4. Escalation Guidelines:
   - Clearly define when and how problems should be escalated based on their category and priority level.

5. Collaboration:
   - Foster collaboration among team members to ensure that the correct category is assigned and that everyone is aligned in their understanding of problem categorization.

6. Consistent Documentation:
   - Document the categorization process within problem records, and ensure that the assigned category aligns with the nature and impact of the problem.

7. Continuous Training:
   - Provide ongoing training and awareness programs to keep the Problem Management team up to date with the categorization criteria and any changes.

Examples of Problem Categories

Problem categories may vary depending on the organization's specific services and requirements. However, here are some common examples of problem categories and subcategories:

1. Hardware Issues:
   - Server Hardware: Problems related to server components like CPUs, memory, or hard drives.
   - Network Hardware: Problems associated with network devices such as routers, switches, or firewalls.
   - Client Hardware: Issues with end-user devices like computers, laptops, and mobile devices.

2. Software Issues:
   - Operating System: Problems related to the underlying operating system on servers or client devices.
   - Application Software: Issues with specific software applications or programs.
   - Database Software: Problems related to database systems or software.

3. Network Issues:

- Connectivity: Problems involving network connectivity, including outages and slow network performance.
- Security: Issues related to network security, such as firewall configurations or intrusion detection.
- Bandwidth: Problems affecting network bandwidth and data transfer rates.

4. Service Issues:
   - Email Service: Problems with email services, including delivery issues or downtime.
   - Web Services: Issues related to websites and web applications.
   - VoIP Service: Problems with voice-over-IP (VoIP) telephony services.

5. Infrastructure Issues:
   - Data Center: Problems affecting data center infrastructure, such as power, cooling, or physical security.
   - Environmental: Issues related to environmental factors like temperature or humidity.
   - Facility: Problems with office facilities that impact IT operations.

6. Application Issues:
   - Performance: Problems related to slow or unresponsive applications.
   - Functional: Issues with specific application functions or features.
   - Integration: Problems stemming from the integration of multiple applications.

7. Security Issues:
   - Cybersecurity: Problems related to cybersecurity, including malware infections or data breaches.
   - Access Control: Issues concerning user access and permissions.
   - Incident Response: Problems associated with the handling of security incidents.

Categorizing problems is an essential practice within the Problem Management process. It ensures that identified issues are organized and prioritized effectively, leading to more efficient investigation and resolution. By following best practices, maintaining clear definitions, and fostering collaboration among team members, your organization can create a well-structured problem categorization system that enhances the overall problem management process.

Prioritizing Problems Using Impact and Urgency

Effective Problem Management involves systematically addressing problems based on their importance and impact on IT services and business operations. To accomplish this, it is essential to prioritize problems accurately. In this chapter, we will explore the significance of prioritizing problems using impact and urgency, and we will provide insights into the process and best practices.

The Significance of Prioritizing Problems

Prioritizing problems is vital for several reasons:

1. Resource Allocation: It helps allocate limited resources efficiently by focusing on the most critical issues first.

2. Mitigating Impact: Prioritization enables organizations to minimize the impact of problems on IT services and business operations.

3. Meeting Service Levels: It assists in meeting service level agreements (SLAs) by ensuring that problems that threaten service quality are addressed promptly.

4. Optimizing Workflow: Problem prioritization streamlines the workflow of the Problem Management team, ensuring that they address problems in the order of their significance.

Using Impact and Urgency for Prioritization

One commonly used method for prioritizing problems is based on the concepts of "impact" and "urgency." Let's understand these two critical factors:

1. Impact:
   - Impact refers to the extent to which a problem affects IT services, business operations, and end-users. It is typically categorized as high, medium, or low and considers the following aspects:
       - Service Availability: Does the problem cause service outages or disruptions?
       - Business Impact: How does the problem impact the core business operations and revenue?
       - End-User Experience: Does the problem affect end-user satisfaction and productivity?
   - High impact problems require immediate attention due to their severe consequences.

2. Urgency:
   - Urgency reflects the need for prompt action to address a problem. It considers factors such as:
       - Time Sensitivity: Is there a time-critical deadline or event associated with the problem?
       - Regulatory Compliance: Does the problem pose a risk of non-compliance with regulations?
       - Business Objectives: How does the problem align with organizational goals and priorities?
   - Urgent problems require immediate attention to prevent escalation or negative consequences.

Prioritization Matrix: Impact vs. Urgency

A prioritization matrix, often depicted as a two-dimensional grid, helps categorize problems based on their impact and urgency. The matrix typically includes four quadrants:

1. Critical (High Impact, High Urgency):

- Problems in this quadrant demand immediate and focused attention. They have the potential to cause significant disruptions to services and business operations.

2. Major (High Impact, Low Urgency):
   - These problems have a high impact on services but are not time-sensitive. They should be addressed in a controlled and planned manner.

3. Minor (Low Impact, High Urgency):
   - While these problems require swift action, they have a limited impact on services and business operations.

4. Trivial (Low Impact, Low Urgency):
   - Problems in this category have minimal consequences and can be addressed at a lower priority.

Best Practices for Prioritizing Problems

To prioritize problems effectively, consider the following best practices:

1. Establish Clear Criteria:
   - Develop clear and well-defined criteria for assessing impact and urgency, ensuring consistency in the evaluation process.

2. Collaboration and Communication:
   - Encourage collaboration between the Problem Management team and other relevant teams, such as Incident Management and Change Management, to gather insights into impact and urgency.

3. Documentation:
   - Document the criteria for impact and urgency assessment in your organization's Problem Management policy and guidelines.

4. Scoring System:
   - Implement a scoring system for impact and urgency to assign numerical values, making the prioritization process more objective.

5. Regular Review:
   - Periodically review and update the prioritization criteria to align with changing business needs and industry standards.

6. Feedback Loop:
   - Establish a feedback mechanism that allows stakeholders to provide input on the impact and urgency of problems.

7. Consistent Training:
   - Ensure that the Problem Management team is trained and kept informed about the impact and urgency assessment process.

8. Automated Tools:

- Consider using problem management software that can automate the impact and urgency assessment process, making it more efficient.

Problem Models and Templates

Problem models and templates are valuable tools in Problem Management that provide structured frameworks for analyzing, documenting, and resolving problems efficiently. In this chapter, we will explore the significance of problem models and templates, their key components, and how to develop and use them effectively.

The Importance of Problem Models and Templates

Problem models and templates are crucial in Problem Management for the following reasons:

1. Consistency: They ensure that problem analysis and resolution follow a standardized and consistent approach, regardless of the complexity or nature of the problem.

2. Efficiency: Templates provide a predefined structure that accelerates the problem-solving process, reducing the time and effort required for problem investigation and resolution.

3. Knowledge Sharing: Problem models and templates serve as repositories of best practices, making it easier to share knowledge and lessons learned within the team.

4. Training and Onboarding: Templates are valuable tools for training new team members, as they provide a clear guide on how to approach problem analysis and resolution.

Key Components of Problem Models and Templates

A well-structured problem model or template should include the following key components:

1. Problem Description:
   - A concise and clear description of the problem, including its symptoms, impact on services, and any relevant context or history.

2. Incident History:
   - A summary of related incidents, including their frequency, duration, and affected services. This section establishes the link between incidents and the underlying problem.

3. Root Cause Analysis (RCA):
   - A structured framework for conducting root cause analysis, which may include techniques like the "5 Whys" or Fishbone diagrams to identify the root causes of the problem.

4. Problem Analysis:
   - A section that outlines the steps taken in the problem analysis process, including data collection, analysis methods, and findings.

5. Resolution Plan:
   - Details of the plan for resolving the problem, including change requirements, workaround implementation, or specific actions that need to be taken.

6. Escalation Procedures:
   - A guide on when and how to escalate the problem to higher levels of expertise or management, including defined criteria and points of escalation.

7. Documentation and Reporting:
   - Guidance on how to document the entire problem management process and generate reports for internal and external stakeholders.

8. Templates for Common Problems:
   - Predefined templates for recurring or common problem types, streamlining the process and ensuring consistent problem resolution.

Developing Problem Models and Templates

To create effective problem models and templates, consider the following steps:

1. Identify Common Problem Types:
   - Analyze historical problem data to identify recurring or common problem types that can benefit from predefined templates.

2. Collaborate with Subject Matter Experts:
   - Work with subject matter experts within your organization to develop and refine problem models and templates. Their insights are invaluable.

3. Standardize the Structure:
   - Ensure that the structure of your problem models and templates remains consistent to promote uniformity in problem analysis and resolution.

4. Document Best Practices:
   - Include best practices and guidelines within the templates to assist problem managers in their decision-making process.

5. Training and Onboarding:
   - Incorporate templates into the training and onboarding processes for new team members to expedite their learning curve.

Using Problem Models and Templates Effectively

To make the most of problem models and templates, consider the following best practices:

1. Tailor to the Problem:

- While templates provide a structured framework, remember to customize them to fit the specific problem at hand.

2. Regular Updates:
   - Periodically review and update problem models and templates to keep them aligned with changing technology and evolving best practices.

3. Knowledge Sharing:
   - Encourage team members to share their experiences and lessons learned using problem models and templates to enhance the knowledge repository.

4. Continuous Improvement:
   - Use feedback from the team to refine and improve problem models and templates continuously.

5. Automation Integration:
   - Consider integrating templates into your problem management software or tools to streamline and automate the problem-solving process.

Examples of Problem Models and Templates

Problem models and templates can vary based on the nature of the problems and the specific needs of your organization. Here are some examples:

1. Server Outage Template:
   - A template for addressing server outages, including predefined steps for root cause analysis, escalation points, and incident history.

2. Software Bug Template:
   - A model for investigating and resolving software bugs, with sections for incident history, RCA, and resolution planning.

3. Network Performance Problem Model:
   - A structured framework for analyzing and resolving network performance issues, encompassing impact assessment, trend analysis, and resolution plans.

4. Security Incident Template:
   - A template for managing and mitigating security incidents, with a focus on impact, urgency, and regulatory compliance.

5. Change-Related Problem Template:
   - A template for problems arising from recent changes, emphasizing the linkage between changes and incidents.

Problem Triage

Problem triage is a pivotal step in the Problem Management process that involves the initial assessment and classification of problems to determine their urgency and priority. Triage helps in efficiently allocating resources and addressing problems based on their impact and criticality. In this chapter, we will explore the significance of problem triage, the key components of the process, and best practices for effective triage.

The Importance of Problem Triage

Problem triage is crucial for several reasons:

1. Resource Allocation: It ensures that limited resources are allocated to address problems that have the most significant impact on IT services and business operations.

2. Timely Resolution: Triage helps in identifying and addressing critical problems promptly, reducing the risk of extended service disruptions.

3. Optimized Workflow: It streamlines the workflow of the Problem Management team by directing their attention to the most urgent and impactful issues.

4. Supporting Service Levels: Triage contributes to meeting service level agreements (SLAs) by focusing on problems that could jeopardize service quality.

Key Components of Problem Triage

An effective problem triage process typically includes the following key components:

1. Problem Identification:
   - The process begins with the identification of problems, often based on incident patterns, user feedback, or automated monitoring alerts.

2. Initial Assessment:
   - An initial assessment is conducted to evaluate the impact and urgency of the problem. This involves gathering relevant information about the problem's symptoms, affected services, and potential root causes.

3. Categorization:
   - Problems are categorized based on their nature, affected services, and business impact, aligning with predefined problem categories.

4. Priority Assignment:
   - Priority levels are assigned to problems based on the results of the impact and urgency assessment. Common priority levels include critical, major, minor, and trivial.

5. Escalation Decision:

- Triage may include a decision on whether the problem should be escalated for further investigation or immediate resolution.

6. Documentation:
   - The results of the triage process, including the assigned category and priority, are documented in the problem record for future reference.

Best Practices for Effective Problem Triage

To ensure that problem triage is conducted efficiently, consider the following best practices:

1. Clear Triage Criteria:
   - Define clear and well-documented criteria for evaluating the impact and urgency of problems. These criteria should align with the organization's specific needs and objectives.

2. Collaboration and Communication:
   - Promote collaboration and open communication between the Problem Management team and other relevant teams, such as Incident Management and Change Management, to gather insights into problem impact.

3. Standardized Triage Process:
   - Standardize the problem triage process to ensure consistency and objectivity in the assessment of impact and urgency.

4. Regular Review:
   - Periodically review and update the triage criteria to adapt to changing business needs, industry standards, and technology advancements.

5. Escalation Guidelines:
   - Define clear guidelines for problem escalation based on priority and impact, specifying when and how issues should be escalated to higher levels of expertise or management.

6. Training and Awareness:
   - Provide training and awareness programs for the Problem Management team to ensure that they understand and apply the triage criteria effectively.

7. Automation Integration:
   - Consider using problem management software or tools that can automate the initial triage process, making it more efficient and reducing human error.

Examples of Triage Criteria

Triage criteria can vary based on organizational needs and priorities. Here are some examples of common triage criteria:

1. Service Impact:

- Assess the extent to which the problem affects the availability and performance of critical IT services.

2. Business Impact:
   - Evaluate the impact of the problem on essential business operations, revenue generation, and customer satisfaction.

3. End-User Experience:
   - Consider how the problem impacts end-users, their productivity, and overall satisfaction.

4. Regulatory Compliance:
   - Assess whether the problem poses a risk of non-compliance with industry regulations or legal requirements.

5. Service Level Agreements (SLAs):
   - Examine whether the problem threatens to breach SLAs and the associated contractual obligations.

6. Resource Availability:
   - Consider the availability of resources, expertise, and tools required for addressing the problem.

Root Cause Analysis and Techniques for Effective Investigation

Root Cause Analysis (RCA) is a systematic and critical process used in Problem Management to identify the underlying reasons for recurring problems and incidents. It goes beyond addressing symptoms to find the fundamental causes, enabling long-term solutions. In this chapter, we will delve into the importance of RCA, key techniques for effective investigation, and best practices for implementing RCA within your organization.

The Importance of Root Cause Analysis

Root Cause Analysis is pivotal in Problem Management for several reasons:

1. Preventing Recurrence: By identifying and addressing the root causes of problems, RCA prevents the recurrence of incidents, minimizing business disruptions.

2. Optimizing Resources: It helps organizations allocate resources more efficiently by focusing on the issues that have the most significant impact.

3. Continuous Improvement: RCA supports a culture of continuous improvement, fostering learning and refinement of processes and procedures.

4. Service Quality: It contributes to maintaining and enhancing service quality, aligning with service level agreements (SLAs).

Key Techniques for Effective Root Cause Analysis

Several techniques and methods can be employed to conduct effective Root Cause Analysis. Here are some key ones:

1. The 5 Whys:
   - This technique involves repeatedly asking "why" to dig deeper into the causes of a problem. By asking "why" five times or more, you can often uncover the root cause.

2. Fishbone Diagram (Ishikawa or Cause-and-Effect Diagram):
   - This visual tool helps in identifying potential causes of a problem by categorizing them into different branches on a diagram resembling a fishbone.

3. Fault Tree Analysis:
   - A systematic and graphical method for identifying the combination of events or conditions that lead to a specific problem or incident.

4. Pareto Analysis (80/20 Rule):
   - This technique focuses on identifying the vital few causes that contribute to the majority of problems. It prioritizes resources for the most impactful issues.

5. Failure Mode and Effects Analysis (FMEA):
   - FMEA assesses potential failure modes in a system, product, or process to determine their effects and prioritize corrective actions.

6. Change Impact Analysis:
   - Assess the potential impact of recent changes on the problem. Changes can introduce new issues or exacerbate existing ones.

7. Brainstorming and Mind Mapping:
   - Collaborative techniques involving team discussions and visual representations to explore possible causes and relationships.

8. Data Analysis and Trending:
   - Analyze historical data and trends related to the problem to identify patterns and correlations.

9. Interviews and Surveys:
   - Gather information from subject matter experts, end-users, and stakeholders to gain insights into the problem's causes.

10. Quantitative Analysis:
    - Use statistical methods to analyze data and determine correlations or causal relationships.

Best Practices for Effective Root Cause Analysis

To ensure that Root Cause Analysis is conducted effectively, consider the following best practices:

1. Team Collaboration:
   - Involve cross-functional teams with diverse expertise to bring a broader perspective to the analysis.

2. Structured Approach:
   - Follow a structured and documented process for conducting RCA to ensure consistency and repeatability.

3. Data Collection:
   - Gather all relevant data, including incident reports, logs, and historical information, to support the analysis.

4. Systematic Documentation:
   - Document the entire RCA process, including findings, potential causes, and the selected root cause, to create a knowledge repository.

5. Time Management:
   - Manage the time spent on RCA effectively to avoid over-analysis and ensure a timely resolution.

6. Continuous Learning:
   - Use RCA as a learning opportunity. Implement preventive measures and share lessons learned with the organization to avoid future incidents.

7. Feedback Loop:
   - Encourage feedback from team members and stakeholders to continuously improve the RCA process.

8. Training and Skill Development:
   - Invest in training and skill development for team members to enhance their analytical and problem-solving capabilities.

Implementing Root Cause Analysis in Practice

To implement Root Cause Analysis effectively in your organization, follow these steps:

1. Define RCA Policies and Procedures:
   - Develop clear policies and procedures that outline how RCA should be conducted, documented, and reported.

2. Train Your Team:
   - Provide training and guidance to your team members on RCA techniques, tools, and processes.

3. Select Appropriate Tools:
   - Use software and tools that support RCA processes and data analysis, such as incident management systems.

4. Assign Responsibilities:
   - Clearly define roles and responsibilities within the RCA team, including a designated leader and subject matter experts.

5. Document Findings:
   - Document the RCA process, findings, and recommended actions in a structured format for future reference and analysis.

6. Implement Preventive Actions:
   - Based on RCA findings, implement corrective and preventive actions to address the identified root causes.

7. Measure Results:
   - Continuously monitor and measure the effectiveness of the implemented actions to verify that they prevent problem recurrence.

8. Knowledge Sharing:
   - Share RCA findings and lessons learned across the organization to prevent similar incidents and encourage a culture of continuous improvement.

Implementing Solutions and Creating Workarounds

In the Problem Management process, identifying the root cause is only the first step. Once the root cause is known, it's essential to implement solutions to prevent the problem's recurrence. Additionally, creating and documenting workarounds can help minimize the impact of problems while long-term solutions are being developed and implemented. This chapter will explore the process of implementing solutions, creating workarounds, and the importance of documenting these actions.

Implementing Solutions

Implementing solutions is the process of taking corrective and preventive actions to address the root causes of problems. This step is crucial for preventing the recurrence of incidents and improving the overall stability and performance of IT services. Here are key steps to consider when implementing solutions:

1. Root Cause Verification: Before proceeding with any solution, ensure that the identified root cause is accurate and well-documented. This step helps avoid implementing incorrect or ineffective solutions.

2. Solution Design: Develop a detailed plan for addressing the root cause, including the necessary changes, updates, or improvements. Ensure that the solution aligns with the organization's goals and standards.

3. Testing: Thoroughly test the proposed solution in a controlled environment to confirm its effectiveness and safety. This step helps avoid unintended consequences.

4. Change Management: If the solution involves changes to IT services or infrastructure, follow your organization's change management process to assess and implement changes.

5. Documentation: Document the implementation process, including the steps taken, test results, and any changes made. This documentation is valuable for future reference and auditing.

6. Monitoring: Continuously monitor the problem and related incidents to confirm that the implemented solution has effectively addressed the issue.

7. Feedback Loop: Establish a feedback mechanism to gather insights from the Problem Management team and end-users. This feedback can help improve the solution and prevent similar problems.

Creating and Documenting Workarounds

While long-term solutions are essential, there are situations where immediate action is needed to minimize the impact of a problem. Workarounds are temporary measures that allow IT services to continue functioning while the root cause is being addressed. Here's how to create and document workarounds effectively:

1. Identify Critical Functions: Determine which IT services and functions are most critical to the organization. These are the ones that require immediate attention.

2. Temporary Measures: Create temporary measures or workarounds to maintain critical functions. These measures should be well-documented and easy to follow.

3. Communication: Communicate the use of workarounds to relevant teams, end-users, and stakeholders. Ensure that everyone is aware of the temporary measures and understands how to implement them.

4. Testing: Test the workarounds to confirm their effectiveness in maintaining critical functions without causing further issues.

5. Documentation: Document the workarounds in a clear and accessible format, such as a knowledge base or incident documentation. Include step-by-step instructions, known limitations, and expected duration of use.

6. Monitoring: Continuously monitor the effectiveness of workarounds and the status of the underlying problem. Update or adjust workarounds as necessary.

7. Feedback and Reporting: Encourage feedback from those using the workarounds. This feedback can help refine the workarounds and improve the user experience.

Importance of Documentation

Documentation is a critical aspect of both implementing solutions and creating workarounds. Here's why it's essential:

1. Knowledge Preservation: Well-documented solutions and workarounds preserve the knowledge gained during the problem management process. This knowledge is invaluable for training, future reference, and audits.

2. Consistency: Documentation ensures that the same solutions and workarounds are consistently applied when similar problems arise.

3. Audit Trail: Documentation provides an audit trail of actions taken during problem resolution, helping organizations demonstrate compliance with policies and standards.

4. Communication: Clear and accessible documentation allows for effective communication with team members, stakeholders, and end-users.

5. Continuous Improvement: Analysis of documentation can identify patterns, recurring problems, and opportunities for process improvement.

6. Efficiency: Well-documented solutions and workarounds save time by eliminating the need to reinvent the wheel when similar problems occur.

Testing and Validation in Problem Management with Change Management Integration

Effective Problem Management goes beyond identifying root causes and implementing solutions. It involves rigorous testing and validation processes to ensure that changes made to address problems do not introduce new issues. Additionally, integrating Problem Management with Change Management is crucial to control and coordinate changes related to problem resolution. In this chapter, we will explore the significance of testing and validation, the integration of Problem Management with Change Management, and best practices for seamless collaboration between these two processes.

The Importance of Testing and Validation

Testing and validation are essential in Problem Management for several reasons:

1. Risk Mitigation: Rigorous testing minimizes the risk of introducing new problems or exacerbating existing ones during the implementation of solutions.

2. Ensuring Functionality: Validation confirms that the implemented solutions or workarounds do not disrupt the functionality of IT services.

3. Compliance and Audit: Documentation of testing and validation processes is crucial for compliance with industry standards and regulations. It also provides an audit trail.

4. User Satisfaction: Effective testing and validation processes help ensure that end-users experience minimal disruption, enhancing their satisfaction.

5. Efficiency: Timely and effective testing minimizes the delay between problem identification and resolution.

6. Continuous Improvement: Insights gained during testing can lead to iterative improvements in solutions and processes.

Integration with Change Management

Integrating Problem Management with Change Management is critical for controlling and coordinating changes related to problem resolution. Change Management provides a structured approach to assess, plan, and implement changes to IT services. Here's why integration is important:

1. Change Coordination: Integration allows for the coordination of changes initiated by Problem Management with planned changes in the organization, minimizing conflicts and disruptions.

2. Risk Reduction: Change Management provides a formal process to assess and mitigate the risks associated with implementing changes. Integrating Problem Management findings ensures that risks related to problem resolution are considered.

3. Communication: Integration fosters clear communication between teams, ensuring that the Problem Management team's findings and recommendations are effectively communicated to the Change Management team.

4. Transparency: Problem Management findings and the associated changes are documented and transparently communicated, enhancing accountability and auditability.

5. Resource Allocation: Integration ensures that resources, including personnel and infrastructure, are allocated efficiently for both problem resolution and change implementation.

Testing and Validation Processes

A well-structured testing and validation process should include the following steps:

1. Test Planning:
   - Develop a test plan that outlines the scope, objectives, and methodologies for testing. Consider the impact on IT services and end-users.

2. Test Execution:
   - Conduct thorough testing of the proposed solutions or changes. This may include functional, regression, performance, and security testing, as well as user acceptance testing (UAT).

3. Validation:
   - Validate that the changes do not negatively impact IT services or end-users. Verify that the problem has been effectively resolved.

4. Documentation:
   - Document the test and validation process, including the results, any issues identified, and actions taken to address them.

5. Approval:
   - Obtain approval from relevant stakeholders, including the Change Advisory Board (CAB) in Change Management, before proceeding with implementation.

6. Communication:
   - Communicate the results of testing and validation to all relevant teams and stakeholders to ensure everyone is informed and aligned.

7. Feedback and Iteration:
   - Use feedback from testing to iterate and refine solutions or changes as necessary.

Best Practices for Testing and Validation

To ensure that testing and validation are conducted effectively, consider the following best practices:

1. Collaboration: Foster collaboration between Problem Management, Change Management, and other relevant teams to coordinate and streamline the testing and validation process.

2. Comprehensive Testing: Include a variety of testing types, such as functional, performance, and user acceptance testing, to comprehensively assess changes.

3. Testing Environments: Maintain separate testing environments that mirror the production environment to conduct controlled testing.

4. Documentation: Maintain detailed documentation of the testing and validation process, results, and any deviations from the expected outcomes.

5. Risk Assessment: Continuously assess the risks associated with changes and ensure that they are addressed through the testing and validation process.

6. User Involvement: Involve end-users in UAT to validate that the changes meet their needs and expectations.

7. Change Scheduling: Coordinate with Change Management to schedule change implementation at times that minimize disruption to IT services and end-users.

Change Management Integration Best Practices

Effective integration of Problem Management with Change Management requires the following best practices:

1. Clearly Defined Roles: Ensure that roles and responsibilities are well-defined, and there is clarity on which team is responsible for what aspects of problem resolution and change implementation.

2. Change Advisory Board (CAB) Involvement: CAB members should review and approve changes initiated by Problem Management as part of the overall change management process.

3. Documentation: Maintain clear and comprehensive documentation of problem management findings, recommended changes, and approvals.

4. Communication: Establish clear lines of communication between Problem Management and Change Management teams, ensuring that relevant information is shared in a timely manner.

5. Change Prioritization: Coordinate with Change Management to prioritize changes related to problem resolution in the change schedule.

6. Collaborative Problem Analysis: Encourage Problem Management and Change Management teams to collaborate during the problem analysis phase to identify changes required for effective problem resolution.

Incident and Problem Relationship - Preventing Recurrent Incidents

In the realm of IT service management, incidents and problems are interconnected in a complex web. Incidents are the visible symptoms that disrupt IT services, while problems are the underlying causes of these incidents. Understanding the relationship between incidents and problems is pivotal for efficient IT operations and for preventing recurrent incidents. This chapter delves into the dynamics between incidents and problems, how to identify recurring incidents, and strategies for preventing them effectively.

Understanding the Incident-Problem Relationship

1. Defining Incidents and Problems:
   - An incident is any event that disrupts or degrades the quality of IT services. Incidents are typically reported by end-users or detected through monitoring systems.
   - A problem, on the other hand, is the underlying cause of one or more incidents. Problems are not always visible and often require investigation to identify their root causes.

2. The Incident Lifecycle:
   - Incidents go through a lifecycle that includes detection, logging, categorization, prioritization, diagnosis, resolution, and closure. These steps are managed by the Incident Management process.

3. The Problem Management Process:

- Problem Management focuses on identifying the root causes of incidents, implementing long-term solutions, and preventing the recurrence of incidents caused by the same underlying problems.

4. Incident-to-Problem Transition:
   - Incidents that exhibit recurring patterns, where the same symptoms or issues reoccur, often trigger the transition to Problem Management. It is at this point that the underlying issue is recognized as a problem.

Identifying Recurring Incidents

Preventing recurrent incidents begins with identifying patterns and trends that indicate a problem's existence. Here are the key steps to identify recurring incidents:

1. Incident Data Analysis:
   - Regularly analyze incident data to identify patterns, commonalities, and the frequency of similar incidents.

2. Incident Reports:
   - Review incident reports and service requests to identify recurring issues, including the number of times a specific issue has been reported.

3. User Feedback:
   - Encourage end-users to provide feedback on recurring issues. User feedback is a valuable source of information for identifying problems.

4. Monitoring and Alarms:
   - Use monitoring systems and alarms to identify repetitive events that may indicate underlying problems.

5. Incident Categorization:
   - Categorize incidents by their type and symptoms to identify clusters of related incidents. Repeated incidents within the same category may indicate a problem.

6. Feedback from Incident Management:
   - Collaborate with the Incident Management team to identify and report recurring incidents that may require investigation by Problem Management.

Preventing Recurrent Incidents

Preventing recurrent incidents is a primary goal of Problem Management. Here are strategies and best practices to achieve this:

1. Root Cause Analysis (RCA):
   - Conduct thorough RCA to identify the root causes of problems. By addressing the underlying causes, you prevent the recurrence of related incidents.

2. Knowledge Sharing:

- Document findings from problem investigations and share this knowledge with the Incident Management team. This empowers them to handle similar incidents more effectively.

3. Proactive Monitoring:
- Implement proactive monitoring and alerting systems that can detect early signs of potential problems. This allows for preventive actions before incidents occur.

4. Change Management Integration:
- Integrate Problem Management with Change Management to ensure that proposed changes address the root causes of problems. Coordinate change implementation to avoid recurring incidents.

5. Defining Workarounds:
- When problems are identified but solutions are not yet available, define and document workarounds. These temporary fixes can help mitigate the impact of incidents until permanent solutions are implemented.

6. Trend Analysis:
- Continuously analyze trends in incident data to spot patterns and address potential problems before they escalate into recurring incidents.

7. Feedback Loop:
- Establish a feedback loop that encourages the Incident Management team to report recurrent incidents to Problem Management promptly.

8. Problem Prioritization:
- Prioritize problems based on their impact and urgency. Focus on high-impact, high-urgency problems to prevent major incidents.

9. Continuous Improvement:
- Use the knowledge gained from problem investigations to improve processes, services, and systems, reducing the likelihood of recurring incidents.

10. User Training and Communication:
- Provide training and communication to end-users and staff to reduce human errors that may lead to recurrent incidents.

Incident-Problem-Change Relationship

The relationship between incidents, problems, and changes is interwoven:

1. Incidents Trigger Problems:
- Incidents often serve as triggers that transition to the Problem Management process when patterns of recurrence are identified.

2. Problems Lead to Changes:
- Root causes identified through problem analysis frequently lead to changes in the IT environment to prevent the problem from recurring.

3. Changes and Incidents:
  - Changes initiated to address problems can potentially lead to new incidents if not properly managed through Change Management. Therefore, coordination between Problem Management and Change Management is essential.

Change Management's Role

Change Management plays a crucial role in preventing recurrent incidents by ensuring that changes implemented to address problems are well-managed. Here's how Change Management contributes to this process:

1. Assessing Change Impact:
  - Change Management assesses the impact of proposed changes on the IT environment, ensuring that they will not introduce new problems or disrupt existing services.

2. Prioritizing

 Changes:
  - Changes related to problem resolution are prioritized, taking into account the impact of the underlying problem and the potential for recurrent incidents.

3. Coordination:
  - Change Management coordinates the scheduling and implementation of changes with Problem Management, minimizing disruptions to IT services.

4. Documentation:
  - Changes related to problem resolution are well-documented, creating a transparent and auditable record.

5. Feedback Loop:
  - Change Management feeds back information to Problem Management, ensuring that the implementation of changes aligns with the root causes identified.

The relationship between incidents, problems, and changes is an intricate web that impacts the stability and continuity of IT services. Identifying recurring incidents is the first step in preventing them. Problem Management, with its emphasis on root cause analysis and solution implementation, is the key to preventing recurrent incidents. Collaboration between Incident Management, Problem Management, and Change Management is essential for effectively identifying, addressing, and preventing problems and their associated incidents. By implementing proactive strategies and maintaining a feedback loop, organizations can reduce the impact of recurring incidents, enhancing service quality and end-user satisfaction.

Knowledge Management in Problem Management - Building a Knowledge Base

In Problem Management, knowledge is a valuable asset that drives efficiency, improves decision-making, and supports the resolution of recurring issues. A well-structured knowledge management system is essential for capturing, organizing, and leveraging the insights gained during problem analysis and resolution. This chapter explores the importance of knowledge management in Problem Management and provides a comprehensive guide to building a knowledge base.

The Importance of Knowledge Management in Problem Management

1. Efficient Problem Resolution:
   - A well-managed knowledge base empowers Problem Management teams to quickly access documented solutions, workarounds, and best practices. This efficiency leads to faster problem resolution.

2. Continuous Improvement:
   - A knowledge base stores valuable insights gained from root cause analysis and problem investigations. This knowledge is essential for identifying patterns, making informed decisions, and implementing long-term improvements.

3. Preventing Recurrent Issues:
   - Knowledge management helps in documenting recurring problems and their solutions. It ensures that the organization does not continually reinvent the wheel when similar issues arise.

4. Enhanced Collaboration:
   - A centralized knowledge base fosters collaboration among teams, as it provides a common repository of information that can be accessed and updated by relevant stakeholders.

5. Onboarding and Training:
   - A well-maintained knowledge base facilitates the onboarding of new team members and supports ongoing training and skill development.

6. Compliance and Auditing:
   - A knowledge base provides an audit trail for problem management activities, which is essential for demonstrating compliance with industry standards and regulations.

Building a Knowledge Base for Problem Management

To establish a comprehensive knowledge base for Problem Management, follow these steps:

1. Identify Key Components:
   - Determine the key components and categories of information that should be included in the knowledge base. This may include solutions, workarounds, incident data, problem records, and best practices.

2. Select a Knowledge Management Platform:
   - Choose a knowledge management system or platform that suits your organization's needs. Popular options include knowledge base software, intranet systems, or document management tools.

3. Capture and Document Insights:
   - Encourage problem analysts and team members to document insights, solutions, and lessons learned during problem analysis and resolution. Ensure that all relevant information is captured.

4. Categorize Information:
   - Organize information into structured categories and subcategories for easy retrieval. This may include categorizing by problem type, IT service, or root cause.

5. Create Clear Documentation:
   - Ensure that all documentation is clear, concise, and well-structured. Use a consistent format, including problem descriptions, root cause analysis findings, recommended solutions, and implementation steps.

6. Version Control:
   - Implement version control to track changes and updates to knowledge base articles. This ensures that the information remains accurate and up-to-date.

7. Metadata and Tagging:
   - Use metadata and tagging to enhance searchability. Assign relevant keywords and tags to articles for easy retrieval.

8. User Access and Permissions:
   - Define access permissions to control who can view, edit, and contribute to the knowledge base. Ensure that team members have the appropriate access levels.

9. Search Functionality:
   - Implement robust search functionality that allows users to find information quickly and efficiently. Consider using full-text search capabilities.

10. Content Validation:
    - Regularly validate and review the content to ensure that it remains accurate and relevant. Remove outdated information and archive articles as necessary.

11. Integration with Problem Management Tools:
    - Integrate the knowledge base with your Problem Management tools and systems, allowing for seamless access to information during problem resolution.

12. Documentation Templates:
    - Develop standardized templates for documenting problems, solutions, and workarounds. Templates streamline the documentation process and ensure consistency.

13. Feedback Mechanism:

- Establish a feedback mechanism that encourages team members to provide updates, corrections, and additional insights to continually improve the knowledge base.

14. Training and User Support:
   - Provide training and support to team members on how to use the knowledge base effectively. Offer resources and guidance on searching for information and contributing content.

Knowledge Base Best Practices

To make the most of your knowledge base in Problem Management, consider the following best practices:

1. Keep it Current: Regularly review and update the knowledge base to reflect changes in the IT environment and emerging insights.

2. Promote Collaboration: Encourage team members to contribute to the knowledge base by sharing their experiences, solutions, and best practices.

3. User-Friendly Design: Ensure that the knowledge base is user-friendly, with an intuitive interface and easy navigation.

4. Integration: Integrate the knowledge base with other IT service management processes, such as Incident Management, Change Management, and Service Request Management.

5. Metrics and Analytics: Monitor knowledge base usage and performance. Collect data on the most frequently accessed articles, user feedback, and areas for improvement.

6. Continuous Improvement: Use knowledge base data and feedback to drive continuous improvement in Problem Management processes and services.

Problem Management Metrics and Key Performance Indicators (KPIs)

In Problem Management, metrics and Key Performance Indicators (KPIs) play a pivotal role in evaluating the effectiveness of the process, measuring progress, and driving continuous improvement. This chapter delves into the importance of tracking and analyzing metrics and KPIs in Problem Management and elaborates on key indicators that provide valuable insights into the process's performance.

The Significance of Metrics and KPIs in Problem Management

1. Performance Assessment: Metrics and KPIs provide a clear picture of how well Problem Management is functioning. They help in assessing the efficiency and effectiveness of problem resolution.

2. Continuous Improvement: By tracking and analyzing metrics, organizations can identify areas for improvement and implement changes that enhance the Problem Management process.

3. Data-Driven Decision Making: Metrics and KPIs serve as the basis for data-driven decision-making. They enable informed choices on resource allocation, process refinement, and problem resolution prioritization.

4. Quality Assurance: Monitoring and measuring performance through metrics and KPIs ensure that Problem Management aligns with organizational goals and service level agreements (SLAs).

Key Metrics and KPIs in Problem Management

1. Problem Closure Rate:
   - Metric: The percentage of problems that have been successfully resolved and closed within a defined timeframe.
   - Significance: Reflects the efficiency of problem resolution and whether problems are addressed in a timely manner.

2. Problem Age:
   - Metric: The average age of open problems or the time problems remain unresolved.
   - Significance: Helps identify aging problems that require attention and highlights potential bottlenecks in the resolution process.

3. Root Cause Identification Rate:
   - Metric: The percentage of problems for which the root cause has been accurately identified.
   - Significance: Assesses the effectiveness of root cause analysis and the quality of problem investigation.

4. Change-Related Problems:
   - Metric: The number and percentage of problems directly related to changes or releases.

- Significance: Indicates the impact of changes on problem occurrence and helps prioritize change management efforts.

5. Repeat Incidents:
   - Metric: The number of incidents related to a specific problem that occurred before the problem was identified and resolved.
   - Significance: Measures the impact of the problem on end-users and the urgency of resolution.

6. Problem to Incident Ratio:
   - Metric: The ratio of problems to related incidents. It helps determine if problems are effectively identified and resolved.
   - Significance: Reflects the relationship between incidents and their underlying problems.

7. Knowledge Base Usage:
   - Metric: The frequency of knowledge base access by Problem Management teams, incident handlers, and end-users.
   - Significance: Measures the effectiveness of the knowledge base and the utilization of documented solutions.

8. Problem Trend Analysis:
   - Metric: The identification of recurring or increasing problem trends over time.
   - Significance: Assists in proactively addressing emerging issues and preventing their escalation.

9. Change Implementation Success Rate:
   - Metric: The percentage of changes initiated by Problem Management that were successfully implemented without introducing new issues.
   - Significance: Evaluates the effectiveness of change management in relation to problem resolution.

10. Customer Satisfaction:
    - Metric: Regularly collected feedback or surveys to measure end-user satisfaction with problem resolution and its impact on service quality.
    - Significance: A satisfied user base is indicative of effective problem management and IT service delivery.

11. Resource Utilization:
    - Metric: The allocation of resources (personnel, infrastructure, and budget) to problem management activities.
    - Significance: Assesses resource efficiency and supports informed resource allocation decisions.

12. Problem Management Cycle Time:
    - Metric: The time it takes to complete the problem management process, from problem detection to resolution and closure.
    - Significance: Measures the efficiency of problem resolution and its impact on service availability.

Setting KPI Targets and Performance Improvement

Once you have identified the relevant metrics and KPIs, it's important to set specific targets and goals. Targets should be based on the organization's objectives, industry standards, and historical performance data. Regularly assess performance against these targets and use the insights gained to drive improvement initiatives. Here's how:

1. Continuous Monitoring: Regularly track and analyze metrics and KPIs to ensure that the Problem Management process is meeting its goals.

2. Root Cause Analysis: If metrics indicate persistent issues, conduct root cause analysis to identify underlying problems within the Problem Management process itself.

3. Performance Feedback: Collect feedback from the Problem Management team, end-users, and other stakeholders to gain insights into process performance and identify areas for improvement.

4. Process Refinement: Based on the analysis of metrics and feedback, refine the Problem Management process to address deficiencies and enhance efficiency.

5. Training and Skill Development: Invest in training and skill development for team members to improve their problem resolution capabilities.

6. Technology and Tools: Evaluate and implement technology, software, and tools that can enhance the efficiency and effectiveness of Problem Management.

7. Collaboration: Foster collaboration with other IT service management processes, such as Change Management and Incident Management, to optimize problem resolution.

Challenges and Pitfalls in Problem Management

Problem Management is a critical component of IT service management, aimed at identifying and addressing the root causes of incidents and recurring issues. While it offers substantial benefits, it also comes with its share of challenges and potential pitfalls. This chapter explores common challenges faced in Problem Management and offers strategies for overcoming them.

Common Challenges in Problem Management

1. Lack of Prioritization: Without proper prioritization, Problem Management teams may spend excessive time on minor issues while more critical problems remain unresolved.

2. Inadequate Resources: Limited resources, including personnel, tools, and budget, can hinder the effective functioning of Problem Management.

3. Resistance to Change: Resistance to process changes or the adoption of new tools can impede the optimization of Problem Management.

4. Inefficient Knowledge Management: Poorly organized or underutilized knowledge bases can lead to delayed problem resolution and the repetition of work.

5. Data Quality and Availability: Insufficient or inaccurate data can hinder problem analysis and the identification of root causes.

6. Complex IT Environments: In complex environments with many interdependencies, identifying root causes can be challenging, especially when issues span multiple systems.

7. Change Management Integration: Poor integration with Change Management can lead to the implementation of changes without thorough problem analysis, potentially causing new issues.

8. Lack of Collaboration: Insufficient collaboration between IT teams, such as Incident Management and Change Management, can hinder effective problem resolution.

9. Communication Issues: Inadequate communication between the Problem Management team and end-users can result in unresolved issues and low customer satisfaction.

10. Resource Constraints: Overburdened staff and limited problem-solving capabilities can slow down problem resolution and hinder effective root cause analysis.

Strategies to Overcome Challenges

1. Prioritization Framework: Implement a clear prioritization framework to focus on high-impact problems first. This ensures that resources are directed toward the most critical issues.

2. Resource Allocation: Advocate for adequate resources, including skilled staff, tools, and budget, to support effective Problem Management.

3. Change Management Communication: Engage in open and transparent communication with Change Management to ensure that changes are aligned with problem resolutions and that potential impacts are considered.

4. Training and Skill Development: Invest in training and skill development for Problem Management teams to enhance their problem-solving and root cause analysis capabilities.

5. Knowledge Management Improvement: Regularly review and enhance the knowledge management system, making it more accessible and user-friendly to encourage contributions and utilization.

6. Data Quality Assurance: Implement data quality standards and processes to ensure that data used for problem analysis is accurate and reliable.

7. Collaboration and Communication: Foster collaboration and open communication between IT teams and stakeholders to streamline problem resolution and prevent recurrence.

8. Feedback Mechanism: Establish a feedback loop with end-users to gather information about recurring issues and areas for improvement.

9. Continuous Improvement Culture: Cultivate a culture of continuous improvement within the Problem Management team, encouraging innovation and process refinement.

10. Metrics and KPIs: Utilize metrics and KPIs to measure performance, identify areas of weakness, and make data-driven decisions to overcome challenges.

Pitfalls to Avoid in Problem Management

1. Focusing Solely on Incidents: Limiting the scope of Problem Management to incidents may lead to the neglect of underlying issues in other IT processes.

2. Neglecting Documentation: Poor documentation practices can result in the loss of valuable knowledge and insights that should be retained for future reference.

3. Overcomplicating Processes: Overly complex processes and tools can hinder efficient problem resolution and increase the likelihood of errors.

4. Ignoring Feedback: Disregarding feedback from end-users and team members can lead to unaddressed issues and low morale within the organization.

5. Failure to Adapt: Failing to adapt to changing IT environments and emerging technologies can render existing problem management practices obsolete.

6. Inadequate Training: Insufficient training and skill development can result in ineffective problem analysis and resolution.

7. Inconsistent Root Cause Analysis: Inconsistent or superficial root cause analysis may result in the recurrence of problems.

8. Lack of Ownership: Problems without clear ownership and accountability are less likely to be resolved effectively.

Continuous Improvement and Optimization in Problem Management

Continuous improvement and optimization are core principles of IT service management, and Problem Management is no exception. This chapter explores the importance of ongoing enhancement in Problem Management, with a specific focus on the post-implementation review (PIR) process as a critical element for optimizing problem resolution and overall service quality.

The Significance of Continuous Improvement

1. Enhancing Service Quality: Continuous improvement ensures that IT services become more reliable and efficient, leading to higher customer satisfaction.

2. Cost Reduction: Identifying and addressing recurring problems can lead to cost savings by reducing the resources needed for incident resolution and problem management.

3. Risk Mitigation: Continuous improvement minimizes the risk of service disruptions and helps identify potential issues before they become major problems.

4. Aligning with Objectives: Regular assessments and refinements ensure that Problem Management aligns with organizational goals and service level agreements (SLAs).

Post-Implementation Review (PIR) in Problem Management

A Post-Implementation Review (PIR) is an essential element of continuous improvement in Problem Management. It serves as a structured process for evaluating the effectiveness of implemented solutions, analyzing the results, and making necessary adjustments. The PIR process involves the following steps:

1. Defining Objectives:
   - Clearly outline the objectives of the PIR. What are you looking to achieve with this review, and what specific areas are you assessing?

2. Gathering Data:
   - Collect relevant data about the problem, its resolution, and the impact of the implemented solution. This may include incident data, user feedback, and performance metrics.

3. Evaluation and Analysis:
   - Assess the results of the implemented solution. Did it resolve the problem as expected, and did it have any unintended consequences?

4. Root Cause Verification:
   - Revisit the root cause analysis to ensure that the identified root cause was indeed the source of the problem and that it was effectively addressed.

5. Documentation Review:

- Examine the documentation related to the problem resolution, including the knowledge base article, incident reports, and problem records.

6. Feedback Gathering:
   - Seek feedback from the Problem Management team, end-users, and relevant stakeholders to understand their perspectives on the solution's effectiveness.

7. Comparative Analysis:
   - Compare the pre-implementation state to the post-implementation state. Has the frequency of related incidents decreased, and have users reported improved service quality?

8. Lessons Learned:
   - Identify lessons learned during the PIR process, including what worked well, what didn't, and what could be improved in future implementations.

9. Adjustments and Recommendations:
   - Based on the evaluation and analysis, make recommendations for adjustments or improvements. These could include further changes, updates to the knowledge base, or process refinements.

10. Documentation and Reporting:
    - Document the PIR findings, recommendations, and actions taken. Report these findings to relevant stakeholders and teams.

Key Elements of Effective PIR

1. Clear Objectives: The PIR should have well-defined objectives and criteria for success to guide the evaluation.

2. Data-Driven: The review should be based on data, metrics, and evidence rather than subjective opinions.

3. Feedback: Gathering feedback from end-users and team members is crucial for a comprehensive evaluation.

4. Root Cause Verification: Ensure that the identified root cause was indeed the source of the problem and that it was effectively addressed.

5. Iterative Process: PIR is an iterative process that fosters ongoing learning and improvement.

Implementing PIR Findings

Once the PIR is completed, it's essential to act on the findings and recommendations:

1. Implementation of Improvements: If adjustments are recommended, ensure that they are implemented promptly and effectively.

2. Knowledge Base Updates: Update the knowledge base with new insights gained during the PIR, including revised solutions and best practices.

3. Training and Skill Development: If the PIR identifies skill gaps, consider providing training and skill development for the Problem Management team.

4. Communication: Share the PIR findings and recommendations with relevant stakeholders and teams, promoting transparency and collaboration.

Automation and Tools for Problem Management

Automation has become an essential component of IT service management, offering numerous advantages in terms of efficiency, accuracy, and scalability. In Problem Management, automation plays a critical role in streamlining the process of identifying, analyzing, and resolving problems. This chapter explores the significance of automation in Problem Management and provides insights into implementing automation effectively.

The Role of Automation in Problem Management

1. Efficiency: Automation streamlines repetitive tasks, reducing the time and effort required for problem identification and resolution.

2. Consistency: Automated processes consistently follow predefined workflows, ensuring uniformity in problem analysis and resolution.

3. Accuracy: Automation reduces the risk of human error, which is especially crucial when identifying root causes and implementing solutions.

4. Scalability: Automation tools can handle a large volume of problems and incidents, making them suitable for organizations with diverse IT environments.

5. Data Analysis: Automation tools can analyze vast amounts of data to identify patterns, trends, and potential root causes.

6. Knowledge Management: Automated systems can contribute to knowledge bases with documentation of resolved problems and their solutions.

Implementing Automation in Problem Management

To implement automation effectively in Problem Management, consider the following key steps and best practices:

1. Define Objectives:
   - Clearly define the objectives of automation in Problem Management. Understand the specific tasks and processes that can benefit from automation.

2. Assess Current Processes:

- Evaluate the existing Problem Management processes and identify areas where automation can add value, such as incident data analysis, root cause identification, and solution implementation.

3. Select Appropriate Tools:
   - Choose automation tools and software that align with your organization's needs. Look for tools that provide scalability, integration capabilities, and a user-friendly interface.

4. Integration with Other ITSM Processes:
   - Ensure that the selected automation tools integrate seamlessly with other IT service management processes, including Change Management and Incident Management.

5. Customization and Configuration:
   - Customize and configure the automation tools to align with your organization's unique requirements and workflows.

6. Data Quality Assurance:
   - Verify the quality and accuracy of data used by automation tools for analysis. Ensure that data sources are reliable and up to date.

7. Testing and Validation:
   - Thoroughly test the automation workflows and processes to identify any issues or glitches. Validate that the automation is functioning as expected.

8. Training and Skill Development:
   - Provide training to the Problem Management team to ensure they are proficient in using the automation tools effectively.

9. Documentation and Knowledge Base:
   - Integrate automation systems with your knowledge base to automatically document resolved problems and their solutions.

10. Monitoring and Reporting:
    - Implement monitoring and reporting mechanisms to track the performance and effectiveness of the automation tools. Use these insights to make improvements.

11. Feedback Mechanism:
    - Establish a feedback loop to collect input from team members and end-users regarding the impact and usability of automation.

12. Continuous Improvement:
    - Continuously assess the performance and functionality of the automation tools. Seek opportunities for enhancements and updates.

Automation Best Practices

1. Start Small: Begin with a manageable scope and gradually expand automation as you gain experience and confidence.

2. Document Automation Workflows: Document the automation processes, ensuring that they are well-documented and easily understood by team members.

3. Change Management: Apply change management principles to the implementation of automation, ensuring that changes are controlled and well-managed.

4. Collaboration: Foster collaboration between the Problem Management team, automation experts, and other ITSM process owners to ensure a coordinated approach.

5. Security: Pay careful attention to the security and data protection aspects of automation tools to safeguard sensitive information.

Summing Up: Key Takeaways

In this comprehensive guide to ITIL Problem Management, we've explored the essential components, best practices, and strategies for establishing and optimizing an effective Problem Management process. Here are the key takeaways from this book:

1. Introduction to ITIL Problem Management:
   - Problem Management is a crucial component of IT service management (ITSM), focused on identifying and addressing the root causes of incidents to prevent their recurrence.

2. Fundamentals of Problem Management:
   - Understanding the core concepts, objectives, and benefits of Problem Management is essential for building a strong foundation.

3. Organizational Readiness:
   - Ensuring that the organization is prepared for Problem Management involves assessing existing processes, resources, and commitment to the practice.

4. Defining Problem Management Processes:
   - Establishing clear and well-documented processes for problem detection, logging, categorization, prioritization, and resolution is fundamental.

5. Building a Problem Management Team:
   - Assembling a skilled and dedicated Problem Management team is crucial, and training and skill development play a key role in team effectiveness.

6. Identifying Key Stakeholders:
   - Recognizing the stakeholders in Problem Management and understanding their roles and interests is vital for collaboration and support.

7. Creating a Problem Management Policy:
   - Developing a comprehensive policy that outlines the objectives, scope, roles, responsibilities, and procedures of Problem Management is essential.

8. Detecting Problems:
   - Implementing effective problem detection methods and tools is the first step in problem resolution.

9. Logging Problem Records:
   - Accurate and detailed problem record logging is vital for effective problem management and root cause analysis.

10. Categorizing Problems:
   - Properly categorizing problems based on attributes such as type, impact, and urgency aids in organization and prioritization.

11. Prioritizing Problems:
   - Utilizing impact and urgency assessments to prioritize problems ensures that resources are allocated to the most critical issues.

12. Problem Models and Templates:
   - Using standardized problem models and templates streamlines problem resolution and documentation.

13. Problem Triage:
   - Implementing a triage process helps quickly assess problems, assign priorities, and determine the appropriate response.

14. Root Cause Analysis:
   - Effective root cause analysis techniques and tools are essential for identifying and addressing the underlying causes of problems.

15. Implementing Solutions and Creating Workarounds:
   - Implementing solutions and workarounds effectively is crucial for resolving problems and preventing incidents.

16. Testing and Validation:
   - Rigorous testing and validation of solutions, along with seamless integration with Change Management, are essential for problem resolution.

17. Incident and Problem Relationship:
   - Understanding the relationship between incidents and problems is crucial for preventing recurrent incidents and improving service quality.

18. Knowledge Management in Problem Management:
   - Building a knowledge base and effectively managing knowledge are vital for enhancing problem resolution and knowledge sharing.

19. Problem Management Metrics and KPIs:
   - Key metrics and KPIs provide valuable insights into Problem Management performance, supporting data-driven decision-making and process improvement.

20. Challenges and Pitfalls in Problem Management:

- Identifying and addressing common challenges and pitfalls is essential for optimizing Problem Management processes.

21. Continuous Improvement and Optimization:
- Post-implementation reviews (PIRs) are critical for evaluating the effectiveness of solutions and driving ongoing improvement in problem resolution.

22. Automation and Tools for Problem Management:
- Automation plays a crucial role in streamlining problem management processes, improving efficiency, and enhancing accuracy.

These key takeaways provide a comprehensive overview of ITIL Problem Management and the steps necessary to establish and optimize this vital component of IT service management. By implementing best practices and leveraging automation, organizations can enhance their problem resolution capabilities, reduce recurring incidents, and deliver more reliable and efficient IT services to end-users.

www.ingramcontent.com/pod-product-compliance
Lightning Source LLC
Chambersburg PA
CBHW062248290526
45794CB00006B/2457